EVANGELISM IN
EVERYDAY LIFE

SHARING
AND
SHAPING
YOUR
FAITH

LYLE
POINTER

JIM
DORSEY

D0111627

Beacon Hill Press of Kansas City
Kansas City, Missouri

Copyright 1998
by Beacon Hill Press of Kansas City

ISBN 083-411-7185

Continuing Lay Training Unit 160.21B

Printed in the
United States of America

Cover Design: Paul Franitza
Cover Photo: Leo De Wys

Library of Congress Cataloging-in-Publication Data
Pointer, Lyle, 1946-
    Evangelism in everyday life : sharing and shaping your faith /
Lyle Pointer, Jim Dorsey.
      p. cm.
    ISBN 0-8341-1718-5
    1. Witness bearing (Christianity)   I. Dorsey, Jim, 1954-
II. Title.
    BV4520.P54   1998
    248'.5—dc21

                                      98-30194
                                      CIP

10   9   8   7   6   5   4   3   2   1

Contents

Preface

At a time when spirituality is of deep interest in North American society, a Wesleyan-Arminian approach to evangelism is worth expressing again in relevant ways. This volume seeks to embrace a variety of methods of evangelism beyond the confrontational style most people have come to accept as the primary way of talking to others about God.

This book attempts to deal with how people are shaped spiritually. Major consideration is given to the work of the Holy Spirit, who chooses to use human relationships as well as Scripture and personal experience as His curriculum in spiritual formation. Another key dynamic includes the context of the church in effectively sharing and shaping faith. God's Spirit has chosen to work through the church to reveal the mysteries of God, namely Christ.

Evangelism has been a fear-producing word for too long. This book seeks to deal with the more common anxieties expressed by believers and allow them to become themselves while engaging in a ministry to seekers. The overwhelming commitment of the authentic Christian is to accomplish the purpose of Jesus, who came to seek and to save the lost. If the church is to accomplish the mission of Christ, we must intentionally and consistently influence others to faith through every available means as a part of our daily routines.

Our hope is that the reader will nurture the lifelong quest in becoming more winsome in sharing and shaping faith in Jesus Christ.

Acknowledgments

Appreciation goes to four ladies: Nina Beegle, who crafted the initial drafts of two chapters; Lori Cable and Cheryl Rains, who typed portions of the manuscript; and Kartha Lynn, who suggested ways by which Christians could pray for unbelievers. I am grateful for my family who encouraged me; to Paula, my wife, who effectively embraces unbelievers and loves them into the church. Thanks to Bill Sullivan, who opened doors for me to express my God-given gifts.

—Lyle Pointer

Also, a special thanks to the staff of The Family Church who live out this book every week:
Barbara Ayala
David Moreno
Greg Munck
Vivian Powell
Suzanne Ryberg

—Jim Dorsey

1

"I Can't Witness—
I'm Afraid!"

If we open our lives and receive God's love, there is only one way that we can express our overwhelming gratitude for such an unmerited gift—by turning that love loose on others.
—H. Eddie Fox and George Morris
Faith Sharing

Lyle

Leading Virgil to the Lord was comparatively easy and natural. He sent a letter to the church where I was associate pastor, saying he wanted to be saved.

I phoned this 42-year-old man and made an appointment to meet him at his apartment one afternoon. He received me graciously, and we visited for a while. When he seemed comfortable with me, I inquired about his relationship with God. He was captivated by the two or three passages of scripture I presented and was soon ready to pray and receive Christ into his life. We prayed, then talked about how to develop and maintain the spiritual relationship he had just begun with the Lord. He exuded confidence in his newfound salvation. We rejoiced together.

As I started to leave, I opened the door and walked into his closet. After untangling my feet from the vacuum cleaner hose, I closed the door, noting the exit door was adjacent. Trying to cover my embarrassment, I said, "With these two doors being so close together, I imagine others have made the same mistake."

"No," he said, "you're the first."

His comment did nothing to alleviate my discomfort. On the

way back to the church I determined I would never tell anybody about that incident.

As I reflected upon it, I realized I was experiencing continual fear about person-to-person encounters on spiritual matters. I thought I had overcome my fear of witnessing. After all, I had received excellent training from four evangelistic organizations and had personally trained over 100 people to share their faith.

Then why was I still apprehensive?

I have concluded God allows us to experience residual fear in this area, never completely removing all anxiety. But why?

Perhaps self-sufficiency would be more a hindrance than a help. If we had no need of Him, each witnessing experience could be just another "notch in our gun"—something good we did. However, the very nature of confronting another person with his or her need requires that we depend upon the One about whom we speak. Our fear compels us to pray for boldness. Paul himself said, "Pray also for me, that whenever I open my mouth, words may be given me so that I will fearlessly make known the mystery of the gospel" (Eph. 6:19).

The early Christians, after being filled with the Holy Spirit, prayed often for boldness, as in Acts 4:29—"Now, Lord, consider their threats and enable your servants to speak your word with great boldness."

Prayer is a pipeline to strength . . .

Prayer is a pipeline to strength that enables us to do what we find humanly impossible. Unfortunately, most believers assume they should never witness until fear is absent, but God's green light is already there. His Spirit supplies the needed courage and boldness to proceed. The sniggling fear that may remain has the benefit of requiring us to exercise our faith in God.

Young Dave, a new Christian, took seriously the scriptural injunction to be a witness. On a city bus one evening he asked Mike, his seatmate, if he had heard of the *Four Spiritual Laws*.

"Not so's I can remember," Mike quipped.

"Well, just listen a minute, and I'll show you," Dave said. It was his first attempt, and he'd decided to play it by ear.

Mike's interest grew, but he kept looking self-consciously from front to side to see whether anyone was watching.

"What do you think, Mike?" Dave asked as they cleared the fourth point. "Would you like to ask Jesus into your life?"

"Huh? Right here in front of everybody? I'd be scared to."

"Well, I felt nervous talking to you too," Dave replied.

Your approach might not be like Dave's, but similarly the witnessing Christian finds the Spirit of God is stronger than the spirit of fear. Personal conflict is not a consideration. Consecration includes giving up the right of self-preservation as we relinquish ourselves to the authority of God.

Overcoming Fear

I wiped my sweaty palms on my pants and tried to calm my pounding heart. I was about to witness to my friend, Damien, whom I had known for some time and whose friendship I valued. It would have been much easier to witness to a little-known acquaintance than to Damien, from whom I had so much to lose.

With thousands of others, I experienced fear at the point of witnessing. How can that fear be overcome? Perhaps it will help to look at some of its causes.

1. *Lack of Confidence.* If we're unsure of our standing with God, we won't be brimming with spiritual confidence. We know we have been saved, but we have some sincere reservations about a few of the claims made for Christianity. We have recurring thoughts that someone with more spiritual maturity should handle these kinds of situations; someone else would be more influential. (To my amazement, 55-year-olds with Ph.D.'s in theology experience these same thoughts.)

You may find it harder to share your faith than someone who is naturally gregarious and assertive. The same principle applies in many areas of life. You may know people who are better at mathematics than you. But you don't use that flimsy reason to deny yourself the benefits of knowing basic math. You tackle it anyway. Just so, we need to trust God and get on with the business of witnessing.

Spiritual maturity is not a prerequisite for effectively sharing your faith. Jesus sent His disciples out two by two before they fully comprehended who He was. In fact, they were ministering before they were Spirit-filled. Statistics indicate that the most effective witnesses are those who have recently come to know Christ—not the long-established members of the church.

While maturity may not be a requirement, personal revival is. Nothing substitutes for the assurance that everything is right between one's heart and God. Even the newest Christian can witness effectively. But trying to tell someone about something one doesn't have is pretty precipitous and is likely to result in failure.

The word "witness" comes from the same New Testament Greek word for "martyr," which is one who lays down his or her life for a cause. This is what Jesus was speaking of when He said, "If anyone would come after me, he must deny himself and take up his cross and follow me. For whoever wants to save his life will lose it" (Matt. 16:24).

2. *Lack of Biblical Knowledge.* We fear someone will ask us questions about the Bible that we can't answer. Yet a person who has studied the Bible for years may not be able to recall upon demand scriptures and references to support what he or she says. We should not assume that we must be able to answer every question with proficiency. The very nature of witnessing precludes having to know everything.

A good friend of mine shared her feelings of inadequacy at this point. She said she overcame her reluctance (but not her fear) by following the "Roman Road" plan of salvation with a few added scripture portions of her own choosing. She had no problem remembering Rom. 3:23—"For all have sinned and fall short of the glory of God"—and from there she had only to turn in her Bible to the scripture verse she had marked in the margin next to that verse, leading her to 6:23, and so with the next verse and the next. Thus, she could easily go from one scripture portion to another, even if her mind went blank. All she had to do was "follow the road" as indicated in the margins of her Bible.

I highly recommend memorizing a handful of scripture verses as an antidote to fear:

Rom. 6:23 explains the need for salvation, the availability of eternal life, and the source of salvation—Jesus Christ.

Eph. 2:8-9 deals with the widespread, mistaken concept that people can work their way into heaven.

John 14:6 assures people that Jesus is the only way to a right relationship with God.

Rom. 5:8 informs the hesitant believer that we need not be "good enough" to receive Christ, for God loved us while we were yet sinners.

Rev. 3:20 provides a beautiful picture of Jesus knocking at our heart's door, wanting to come in.

While these verses don't answer every question people may have, a witness testifies only to what he or she knows from sight, hearing, or experience.

3. *Lack of Know-How and Experience.* If we have not been adequately exposed to various techniques for witnessing, we may feel we simply don't have a starting point from which to begin. Or, perhaps anger, indifference, or discourteous responses from people have made us feel we are not prepared.

By age 16 I had been trained in three methods of evangelism. The instructors made it sound so easy, but somehow the certificate for completion of class work did not provide the inner, quiet spirit I had hoped for when I enrolled. I was 23 before I was able to begin putting into practice what I had learned. It was after a man took me calling and showed me how that I began to witness. While I don't use the method he used, his modeling gave me the boldness to proceed.

Fear caused by lack of know-how can be overcome largely by choosing a plan, technique, or method of evangelism that seems most appropriate. While the "canned" approach is often ridiculed, it has been proven that some plan is better than no plan.

Dwight L. Moody, after preaching on witnessing, was accosted by a woman who informed him that she did not agree with his method of evangelism. "Well, I'm not entirely satisfied with it myself," he said. "Tell me—what method do you use?"

"Well," she said, "I don't have one, but—"

"Ma'am, I think I like my method better than yours," he replied.

Having a plan is tantamount to using a map to get from one place to another. Without it we can easily get sidetracked and end up on a bypath to the wrong place, or on a dead-end road.

I have observed that without some kind of training with a specific plan, most people do not share their faith with any regularity. Those who witness regularly and dynamically rarely use a prescribed method, but they started with one. While the theoretical arguments against the "canned" approach are convincing, practical application seems to mandate initial training in a planned method.

4. *Possibility of Failure.* "What if I drive them farther away from God?" a Sunday School teacher asked. "I might be responsible for their being lost." She chose to risk their destiny in hell by neglect rather than to sow seeds of the gospel by faith.

It is highly improbable anyone has ever been consigned to an eternal hell because someone dared witness to them! Certainly God must have thought of that possibility before He commanded us to witness. Yet He has entrusted something as fragile and eternal as a human soul into the care of fearful, fledgling Christians. God will most likely take what appears to be a human failure and turn it into a phenomenal advancement of the gospel. That's what happened to young John in his first pastorate.

He has entrusted fragile, eternal souls into the care of fearful, fledgling Christians.

John was on call one night when Jean was brought to the hospital by ambulance. She had a serious hemorrhaging problem. "I'm afraid I'm going to die," she told the pastor. With her permission, he presented a simple plan of salvation and prayed with her. She seemed responsive.

Later, when she was well, he visited her at her home. He was received rather coldly and given to understand that she had her own church and her own pastor. "I've been confirmed, and I'm satisfied," she claimed.

Standing at her door, he said, "I don't know what happened at your confirmation, but I do know that if you don't truly repent and confess your sin to God, you'll go to hell." Then he departed as she closed the door on him.

"I guess I really blew that one," he thought. But 10 years later, after he had moved to another state, a letter came to the pastor from that same lady.

"When I closed the door on you that day," she wrote, "I fell against it, trembling and sobbing. I knew what you said was true, and I couldn't get away from it. Thanks to you and to Jesus, I am now a true, born-again Christian!"

God's primary method of delivery is through human beings, and we must leave the results to Him.

God's primary method of delivery is through human beings. Remember the first time you dived off a diving board? All kinds of "what-ifs" bounced around in your head, but you finally said to yourself, "Here goes, whether I live or die!" The hesitancy to fail may indeed be an unearthing of personal pride. We are to give up our lives for His sake.

5. *Social Disapproval.* We don't want to lose a friend or alienate a family member by witnessing. We want people to like us. Though church growth studies show the most influential persons in bringing people to church and to Christ are friends and family members, statistics mean nothing to the panic-stricken heart of the potential witness.

Do we really deal with the root cause of our fear to witness? How real to us is the fact we are not our own, that we have been bought with a price? How absurd to claim to belong to the Lord Jesus and yet be concerned about how we appear to people who hate Him! We are not apt to get their vote of confidence anyway.

The early disciples prayed for boldness to withstand an unprecedented array of evil against them. They were victorious because they understood the magnitude of the God about whom they witnessed.

If we do not recognize ourselves as witnesses of the *victory* of Jesus Christ on the Cross, we will always be intimidated by the threat of opposition. We must realize in all these opposing things "we are more than conquerors through him who loved us" (Rom. 8:37), because He "did not give us a spirit of timidity, but a spirit of power, of love and of self-discipline" (2 Tim. 1:7).

Light is effective in darkness. If we want to witness, we will have to penetrate a darkened world.

2

Do Unchurched People Want to Talk About God?

Jesus wanted His followers to obey Him. . . . And in receiving His Spirit they would know the love of God for a lost world. . . . The disciples understood they were . . . responding to the One that loved them, and Who was willing to give of Himself for them.
—Robert Coleman
The Master Plan of Evangelism

Jim

I rang the doorbell and nervously adjusted my tie. This would be my first attempt at evangelism in my fledgling assignment as a new senior pastor. After Lucy opened the door and introductions were made, she called for her husband: "Come meet the pastor of the new church starting up the street."

Since we had no appointment, Richard seemed reluctant to come to the living room, but he politely shook my hand. It really came as no surprise later when he finally said to me, "Look—church is OK for Lucy. She's the one in our house who goes to church. It's all right with me if she goes, but don't expect me to be there."

Not the kind of response on a first visit that fires up your enthusiasm for evangelism! I still remember the sinking feeling in my heart when Richard had finished his statement. My head said to get up and leave, but my heart wouldn't give up so easily.

Many times when faith becomes frozen in fear, our expectations may have been unrealistic. By expecting the unreasonable, we become overanxious and afraid. Some of the more common fears that have plagued me in sharing faith are as follows:

Thinking others have no interest. Whether they say they are uninterested, like Richard did, or act like they are, we should know better. Many times our impressions of their disinterest reflects our own personal fear of rejection. Seeds of truth take time and nurture to germinate to life. Yet sometimes we expect others to embrace our message of faith the very first time we speak to them.

Instead, accept the notion that we may be planting ideas of truth and the seeds of the gospel that God's Spirit will later cultivate to life in their hearts. Or, to use another description, as we are the savory salt, eventually they will develop a thirst for the Living Water.

We don't want to hurt our friendship. At times we feel afraid to share our faith because we don't want to negatively impact our friendships. But again, this fear grows primarily from another unrealistic expectation: We believe we must argue, debate, rationalize, pressure, or convince our seeking friends to embrace faith against their own will. The misnomer is that faith sharing is a manipulative hard sell and that we are force-feeding truth to people who are deeply resistant. That's just not the case.

Jesus taught us to talk to those who are the most receptive to the truth. He said, "The fields . . . are white . . . to harvest" (John 4:35, KJV). Everywhere there are overly ripe fields with people who are looking for spiritual answers and faith that work in everyday living.

Everywhere there are people who are looking for spiritual answers and faith that work in everyday living.

Our Lord discouraged His disciples from trying to take faith to those who openly fought against the truth. He taught that our task was to be *living witnesses* of truth—not "legal prosecutors" of truth!

We are commanded to speak "the truth in love" (Eph. 4:15) yet to be "harmless as doves" (Matt. 10:16, KJV). Sharing faith is an invitation to enter into a mutual journey for truth. It is highly relational, offering encouragement and insights for the next step toward authentic faith. Rather than hurting a friendship, this kind of concern enriches relationships to higher levels of understanding and communication. This kind of compassion is sensitive to the questions and needs of others, partnering with God's Spirit to impact lives with genuine faith.

Both the biblical record and all we know of the Christian experience teach us that faith sharing and shaping occur in the context of personal interaction. No one ever comes to personal faith in Christ apart from the influence of another believer—one just like you! Every believer can trace his or her spiritual journey by the relational milestones of key faith-shaping people in his or her life. Genuine faith does not injure friendships—it enriches them!

These fears and dozens of others are rooted in half-truths and overly ambitious expectations. Sometimes we're fearful to share faith because we don't want to "say the wrong thing." Again, we should not expect to share faith in just one conversation and immediately change everything a seeker believes. The credibility of a consistent lifestyle provides the strength for faith sharing. For many in our secular society, the arguments for the head are not nearly as impressive as the attitudes of the heart. Most seekers prefer we honestly say, "I really don't know a good answer to that question, but let me think about it. We'll talk it over some more later."

The credibility of a consistent lifestyle provides the strength for faith sharing.

If we expect to be the resident expert of the Bible, "the answer man or woman" to all the perplexing questions of life, our fears in sharing faith will only grow. If we are transparent and honest about our own journey of faith and we communicate in a spirit of concern, seekers will respond positively to our authenticity.

Rather than look at all the fears in sharing faith and examining how they reflect our unrealistic expectations, let's take a more practical approach in dealing with this topic. Let's walk through some basic steps in learning to overcome your fears in sharing faith with others.

Pray about your fears in sharing faith.

As simple as it sounds, prayer proves to be a powerful antidote for fear. The psalmist described this process when he wrote,

"I sought the LORD, and he answered me, and delivered me from all my fears" (Ps. 34:4).

A couple of weeks ago after leading a Bible study, my wife came home with a new verse. One of the women in her group said she had found a new "911 number" for emergencies. It was Ps. 91:11, which reads, "For he will command his angels concerning you to guard you in all your ways." That kind of round-the-clock protection has a way of caring for all our fears and concerns. Faith frees us from fear.

2. Plan what to say in advance.

One of the homework assignments for our new members is to write out a three-sentence testimony. The first sentence is to describe what their lives were like before they put their faith in Christ. The second sentence describes when and where they received Christ into their lives and trusted Him as Lord. The third sentence is to describe the difference faith in Christ has made in their lives.

Those three simple sentences form the framework for a dynamic personal testimony. While this is primarily a testimony to one's personal relationship with Jesus Christ, it also serves as an excellent plan of what to say initially in sharing our faith.

We are instructed to "always be prepared to give an answer to everyone who asks you to give the reason for the hope that you have" (1 Pet. 3:15). By thinking through the reasons for faith and how it has impacted your life, you can share the reasons why you believe. And people want to know that. In fact, seekers are more interested in your personal story of faith than in a long theological explanation on why you believe like you do. They will identify with special moments when the Lord has spoken to you, or unusual answers to prayer. They will be moved by how God used a crisis and problem to get your attention or brought a key person into your life at just the right time. As you share your "ah-ha moments," the Lord can use your spiritual journey to shape faith in the lives of others.

3. Prepare a list of friends and family.

I'm continually amazed at how faithfully God's Spirit assigns seekers to believers. He burdens our hearts for others in spiritual need. We begin to have unique opportunities to share and shape faith in their lives, sometimes in the most unexpected ways. And one helpful step in sharing faith is to develop a list of people you would like to reach.

One of my pastor friends, Wes Williams, used an annual Sunday in his church for preparing his congregation in this important step of faith. In the bulletin was a form to be completed by each believer called "My Ten Most Wanted." Each member and believer was encouraged to prayerfully consider who would be their "Ten Most Wanted" to reach for Christ. By becoming more aware of these seekers in our lives, we are also better prepared to share our faith when the opportunities arise. Once the list is completed, we can pray specifically for these individuals. We can ask the Lord for the right words to say to them when the subject comes up. We can also be ready for the right time and place to share our faith.

Not long ago, one of our newer members sent me the following E-mail message:

I've had the occasion to discuss the idea of God with a woman at the office. An older woman, she was raised in the Jewish faith and, due to family tragedies and personal failures, has decided and firmly believes that there is no God.

She has been involved in some protracted legal issues that resulted in a negative comment on her credit history. She has been unable to clear her credit report and faced the possibility of losing an opportunity to purchase a new house she had been dreaming about. I listened as she lamented her situation, sympathizing but unable to offer any real advice. I told her I'd pray, to which she replied, "There is no God. There is no God. . . ."

Today she was informed that her credit records have been swept clean, clearing the way for the house purchase. Upon learning of this, I took the immediate opportunity to visit her and remind her of my prayers. She looked up from her desk, smiled, paused for a second, and then said softly, "Thank you." Maybe it worked and maybe it didn't, but I think that a simple expression of concern by someone certainly

We sow the seeds, then trust God for results.

helped her feel a little better . . . and perhaps resulted in a crack in her armor.

After we have sown the seeds of truth, we can leave the results to the faithfulness of God. Sometimes when people say "no," they actually mean "not yet."

Partner with other believers for faith sharing.

The scriptures are full of admonitions for partnerships in prayer and ministry efforts. Jesus promised in Matt. 18:19 that "if two of you shall agree on earth as touching any thing that they shall ask, it shall be done for them of my Father which is in heaven" (KJV).

Faith is best shared and shaped in the context of a community of faith. When believers in a local church begin to partner together to impact their friends and family for Christ, exciting things begin to happen.

Local churches can agree together to provide a safe place where seekers can come and process their questions. Faith partners can commit themselves to helping each other reach loved ones for Christ. When a local fellowship enlists such partnerships for sharing and shaping faith, results seem to multiply!

That's how I ended up talking with Richard and Lucy that day in our first visit. We discussed what kind of church this was going to be and how we needed everyone to get involved to make it work. I said, "Richard, I'm looking for a few volunteers who will hand out the programs each Sunday and welcome people to our new church. I know you don't plan to come every Sunday, but think about helping us as a greeter."

I'll never forget when Lucy drove up to church for our very first Sunday service. Richard got out of the passenger's side and walked straight to me. "Where are the bulletins I need to hand out?" he asked. At the end of the service that day, he was the very first one to come forward to receive Christ into his life—for the first time, at age 73! In my years as pastor there, Richard never missed a Sunday.

Faith sharing and shaping in the local church is an adventure. As people are enlisted and involved, members form partnerships and share a vision. God honors such faithfulness with His blessings of fruitfulness.

3

Where Is God in the Work of Evangelism?

Long before we were able to identify God's presence or focus on His deeds, He was active. No one is a stranger to God. Long before we ever move toward Him, God has already moved toward us. Even when we do respond, He makes the response possible.
—Al Truesdale and Bonnie Perry
A Dangerous Hope

Lyle

A member of Jake's family had attended church the previous Sunday. I returned the visit one afternoon about suppertime. Jake answered the door and invited me in. Conversation came easily. He told me of his family origin, how they had moved to the city four years earlier, about their church background. He explained about their present church involvement—how they were sporadic in their worship attendance and hesitant to make a commitment to any particular church. He talked about his belief that there are many ways to God and that no one single church has a corner on truth.

I asked Jake about his own spiritual life. He noted he was usually trying to do his best, although he knew he fell far short of what God expected. He wanted to be a better person and a better Christian. Our conversation flowed back and forth, and he expressed a longing to be nearer to God.

My experience with Jake contrasted with my meeting with Ann. Ann had attended church at the invitation of one of the altos in our choir when the choir was presenting a musical. She said she had enjoyed the service and complimented the choir and the music director for the fine production. She mentioned she attended church mostly on special occasions such as the one at our church. Upon my questioning her about her church background, she became tense. Her comments were short and guarded. I inquired as to her feelings about her days growing up in church. She changed the subject. Later on I said, "When I was a boy, I went to Vacation Bible School and summer camps. Did you also have those experiences?"

"Yes," she responded. "But I don't feel good about what happened in our church when I was a teenager."

"Are you comfortable talking about what took place?"

"No," she responded. "I don't want to talk about it."

"I sense you had a difficult experience. If there's ever a time when you'd like to talk about that or what your future relationship with God might be," I offered, "I'd be happy to discuss that with you."

"Thanks," she said, "but not now."

The witness must understand where the pre-Christian is on the journey.

Jake and Ann are at different places in their spiritual lives. God has undoubtedly been working with both of them, but they've chosen to respond in different ways. *The Christian witness must understand where people are in their spiritual journeys.*

All people, however, have spiritual longings. God made us each that way. Sometimes we imagine those longings to be simply of human origin. But God places those desires within the human heart. Those longings can become sources of spiritual openness. Let's examine some of those human desires.

Each person has a need for hope. Without hope, people give up, quit progressing, and in extreme cases commit suicide. The longing for hope is addressed by a relationship with God. He promises a bright future. He accompanies us on the way. For the person who believes God to be loving, good, and caring, hope always thrives. Apart from God, despair reigns.

Another drive within the human spirit is success. The urge to achieve, to accomplish, to create, and to find fulfillment pushes humans. Generations before Christ, God understood that strong drive and promised success to those who would live according to His Word (Josh. 1). God reveals himself to be an accomplice in the drive to success. He facilitates the pursuit of fulfillment. He also directs an individual to seek Him out as a Companion on the journey to fulfillment.

People long to be free. East Germans were impaled on the Berlin Wall in their pursuit of freedom, a testimony to the human need for liberty. God has always appealed to the longing for liberty. He said truth is a way to freedom.

There is also a desire for forgiveness. Relationships that are broken cause discomfort until restoration comes. The announcement of forgiveness brings satisfaction to the soul. Repeatedly the Scriptures tell us: forgiveness is available through Jesus Christan.

Akin to forgiveness is the desire for acceptance. Acceptance speaks of friendship and closeness. God's acceptance brings hope and encouragement to the human soul. A close relationship with God reflects a healthy drive. Scripture speaks of this inner drive for relationship with the themes of family and offers to dine with God. God's Word is resplendent with "Welcome home" offers.

Yet another longing is for healing and wholeness. While physical healing is a theme of the Bible, spiritual healing is a primary concern. People want to feel complete and healthy. Sin's damage leaves one desiring divine intervention. The aching heart reflects God urging people to move closer to Him.

The Holy Spirit works through the transitions of life. The witness is also to discern the workings of the Holy Spirit in the pre-Christian. The Holy Spirit works through the normal transitions of life. For example, the teenage years are filled with abrupt changes physiologically, socially, educationally, mentally, and spiritually. The Holy Spirit uses this time. Research shows people accept Christ during their teenage years more than at any other point in life.

College is a time of transition. A young adult often leaves home and makes life choices regarding vocational pursuit and even a spouse.

Marriage, the arrival of a baby, the empty nest, and retirement are other occasions in which the Spirit of God deals with people about the implications beyond these temporal occasions. Natural events are used by God to draw us to himself. *The wise proclaimer of the gospel is alert to the changes in the lives of people.* The stability of God is always a great theme when people are struck by the vicissitudes of life.

Not only are transitions a time of openness, but so are crises. Loss highlights our vulnerability and creates openness to the gospel. Death, divorce, financial crisis, job transition, and a multitude of other circumstances can make us recognize we are not in control. We lose hope and long for someone to provide strength and support. We desperately need someone to help us with the pain. These circumstances commonly provoke us to consider the spiritual when previously we may not have given God a thought. God is a wonderful resource, especially for people in need.

God's world speaks volumes. Underlying the variety of personal life experiences, God speaks to all people through nature. Creation announces, "This is what God is like." Even His "invisible qualities—his eternal power and divine nature—have been clearly seen" (Rom. 1:20). God's world has spoken words to people. His creation calls in descriptive cries to us, His creatures.

Pastors and Sunday School teachers frequently hear accounts of persons sensing God as they view open meadows, meandering streams, majestic mountains, or smashing waves of ocean surf. (These reports may sometimes be given as reasons for missing church!) Indeed, God declares himself in a variety of ways. His messages are convincing and compelling.

A Christian worker, Jeanette, visited the home of Sue, who had attended church the previous Sunday. Sue and her daughter invited her to join them in the living room, where they had been chatting and eating popcorn. Jeanette asked Sue, "Do you think much about God?"

"Oh, yes!" Sue said as she selected a hard kernel from the bowl. "In fact, I just mentioned to my daughter how it's a miracle for popcorn to become so soft and tasty."

Jeanette picked up on nature's revelation as the prompting

of God. She used the change in popcorn as an illustration of God's redeeming work in people. She led Jeanette and her teenage daughter to Christ that evening.

How does the Holy Spirit work in the life of a pre-Christian? He deals with the thought life of people. Some thoughts may appear at first to be simply random. Then they take on an orderliness. The pre-Christian begins to recognize the consistency, even though the thoughts may come only occasionally. The thoughts prompted by the Spirit then begin to be tied together.

Insight into human nature, into God's working, into a relationship are seen to have their source in God. A common occurrence is to be blind to the source of these thoughts. Being oblivious to God's work is the experience of not only the pre-Christian but the Christian as well.

For example, in Acts 10 the Holy Spirit is dealing with Peter regarding his prejudices against the Gentiles. When Cornelius, a Gentile with an interest in God, sends his messengers to recruit Peter to hold a revival, then and only then does Peter make the connection. The insight into the expansion of the gospel and the inclusion of the Gentiles in the plan of God captures Peter's mind, changes his behavior, and makes him an advocate for including those who were formerly outcasts.

The Holy Spirit convinces people of sin (John 16:8-15). It's been popular to talk about conviction—the work of God's Spirit to create a sense of guilt within the unbeliever. This is one way God works. With the rise of moral relativity, however, people are changing the rules. For example, many excuse adultery as not being a sin. Morality is measured by legality. If a behavior is legal, although it may not be moral, people justify what might be very damaging to others—after all, the behavior is legal. Therefore, they conclude that it's all right.

Some people don't understand conviction. I went to visit Evelyn, who was residing in a retirement home. She was alert and reflective; sincere and earnest. As she described her life, her health, and her feelings, she mentioned she feared losing her mind. Surprised by her observation, I asked more questions. She began to describe a recurring sense that things were not right inside. She looked over her past with deep regret and remorse. Feeling she needed reassurance, I started to minimize her feelings as being merely a review of the past, over which we could do nothing. She bristled slightly at my cavalier comment. Catching on that I had made a mistake, I asked her for permission to explore some specifics in her life. She consented. I asked her if some of her regrets would be related to what she felt was her wrongdoing. She lit up, responding eagerly with a yes. Just as quickly as she affirmed her sin, her face clouded with a heavy sense of responsibility and sadness. I asked her if she had ever heard of the term "conviction." She replied she had not. I explained how God reminds us of our sins so we'll come to Him for forgiveness.

She said, "Why, I didn't know God did that. But I'm confident that's what's happening."

He offers relationship through accepting His forgiveness.

My response to her was along these lines: "I have good news—and some *more* good news. First, you're not losing your mind. In fact, your mind is functioning very well, for the Holy Spirit is able to deal with you about your past. And He's calling you into a relationship with Him that's begun by accepting His forgiveness. Your relationship with Him need not be clouded by fear, anxiety, or guilt."

In a direct conversation with God, Evelyn prayed for His forgiveness. She was confident He had granted her request.

Another feature of the Holy Spirit's work is this: He convinces people that judgment will come. People sense the anger of God—His disapproval. That's the negative aspect of the Holy Spirit's work. It is nonetheless a necessary work by Him. He does not allow us to be comfortable with our wrongdoing. The inevitable judgment our sins bring causes Him to call attention to the consequences of wrongdoing.

No person is very far away from the conviction that what a person sows, he or she is going to reap. No one is immune to that ongoing universal principle.

God convinces people to live right. People admit to the presence and the desirability of good in the world. Even people who acknowledge they are terrible sinners try simultaneously to overcome their sin with an abundance of good deeds. Acts of

kindness are noted by people universally. Right living is basical-
ly winsome and attractive. When a person's life is ended here on
earth, those who grieve point to the good done. The work of God
unendingly reaffirms right living. God and humans both ap-
plaud kind words, acts of mercy, and demonstrations of love.

Church services, preaching, and Communion have for hun-
dreds of years been called "means of grace," methods God uses
to communicate His love and mercy. In a re-
cent survey, more than 77 percent of churchgoers said that Sunday morning worship
services had been very influential in their
salvation, and more than 64 percent said
that a Sunday School class was very important to their conversion experience. These
findings point out the value of encouraging
people to involve themselves in the life of a local fellowship of
believers. God still uses people to accomplish His purpose of redemption.

God uses people to accomplish His redemption in others.

God also uses dreams and apparitions. Historically Jews
and Christians have believed God intervenes in the subcon-
scious. He operates at some subliminal level, not altogether de-
finable but nonetheless real. Just this week my daughter told of
having a dream in which Christians were ascending in the Rap-
ture but she herself was not leaving gravity's hold. She became
panicky. When it looked as though everyone else would leave
her behind, she began to "lift off." (She admits that in order to
catch up, she had to shove off with her right foot.) From her
dream she acknowledged a fear of being left behind. She wanted
to go along, to be included, to be with God and His family.
Dreams are not unusual or infrequent in their spiritual meaning.
People will discuss their dreams and their spiritual interpreta-
tions. God is obviously at work, even while we sleep.

Apparitions are sightings that are unusual and capture the
human mind and spirit. On April 19, 1995, a lady was driving on
the freeway heading toward Oklahoma City Center. She observed clouds appearing as angels. Suddenly, and with rapid
movement, the clouds seemed to surge toward downtown Oklahoma City. She felt and heard some noise. Only later did she discover the angels were flying to the site of the Alfred P. Murrah

Federal Building bombing. God is at work in unusual ways to move people spiritually, and His methods are as varied as the personalities He's given us. *The task of the witness is to discern the workings of the Spirit in the lives of pre-Christians.*

God is indeed at work in unusual ways to move people spiritually. Our study of the spirit world is in its initial stages. God is working in a variety of ways.

The Christian witness is to become an agent of the divine in the life of the pre-Christian. We connect the divine workings with the spiritual longings of people. In the New Testament this principle was applied by Philip, the lay evangelist who was used by God to minister to an Ethiopian. The Ethiopian was reading the Bible but not understanding what was meant. He was seeking to understand God through the words of a prophet. Philip took the opportunity to explain Christ to a man who was thirsting to know more.

One of the temptations of the Christian is simply to go around talking about God. The assumption is that God will honor whatever is spoken. This philosophy overlooks the idea that evangelism is intentional and is intentionally connected with the needs of people.

For example, I was visiting with Frenchie, a 67-year-old preacher's kid. The first day we were talking, he began to pour out the pain from his teenage years. He had seen hypocrites and caustic people in his church. Their duplicity angered him even now. He spoke with harsh tones. His body stiffened with anger. He condemned the church. He separated himself from Christ and excused his sinful behavior on the basis of the ungodliness of church people.

After his anger had lessened some, I asked, "Have you ever seen anyone really live the life of godliness?"

"Oh, yes," he responded. "My father was a wonderful man of God—" As tears began to fill his eyes, his voice broke with emotion.

"That answers a lot of questions, doesn't it?" I observed.

A few things worthy of note happened in that interview. First, someone listened to Frenchie's pain. He had a need to express his sufferings. He also felt the need to exonerate his dad, who had been misunderstood and abused verbally. The godly example of his dad, as a model of holiness, connected with a God who was real and winsome. Within 10 weeks Frenchie told his pastor he had accepted the Lord.

The witness skillfully discerns the prevenient workings of the Holy Spirit. As we discern God's work, we're able to act as a spiritual guide. With God's leading, we connect the divine workings with the spiritual longings of the pre-Christian. The gospel is communicated effectively. This is the work of the Kingdom!

4

"God's Been Talking to Me About Witnessing"

You are the light of the world. A city on a hill cannot be hidden. Neither do people light a lamp and put it under a bowl. Instead they put it on its stand, and it gives light to everyone in the house. In the same way, let your light shine before men, that they may see your good deeds and praise your Father in heaven.

—Matt. 5:14-16

Jim

Faith shapes like light shines!

Genuine faith influences others. Jesus taught us this truth when He described faith as a candle in the darkness. The smallest candle will always impact its darkened environment. Conversely, no darkness is ever strong enough to put out even the smallest flickering light. Faith shapes like light shines!

Jesus sensed how intimidating sharing our faith can be. Yet He gave us the metaphor of the candle for our encouragement. The light of a candle is not better protected under the safety of a mixing bowl, He said. In fact, when a candle is covered it tends to flicker and go out. To shield and cover goes against the very nature of light. Its function is to fill the place where it is. Faith, just like light, will diminish if concealed or hidden. That's why Jesus said we put a candlestick on a stand where its light can fill the whole room. Authentic faith stands out to anyone in "the dark."

Inside the heart of the Christian is a genuine desire to share faith with other people. The source of that longing does not always begin with Sunday morning preaching, the Bible, or the modeling of other Christians. These factors, the church community and other influences, may direct attention to this spiritual endeavor, but faith has within its very nature the tendency to impact and influence its environment. There are several sources that motivate us to share our faith with others around us. Let's consider some of them.

Lyle

God stirs our hearts to share our faith.

God himself instigates this interest within us. His Spirit even assigns us specific people who need to know Him, as our personal "faith projects." And the origin of His work begins in the relationship He offers to us. God's love for us and His command to love others motivate us to witness. Love by its nature includes others. It reaches out and brings other people in. God's love wells up within us, bubbles over, spills out on others.

God's Spirit will assign us specific people.

This was evident with two senior adults I knew who had been recently widowed. One Sunday morning I spoke to the gentleman, asking him how he was. Preoccupied, he didn't respond right away. But the lady with him spoke up, saying, "He's fine. And so am I"! They were experiencing "the joy of the journey" in their faith. And their delight in their faith was quickly and clearly evident. They wanted other people to join in the celebration.

This is not unlike the newborn Christian and his or her eagerness to tell of this new relationship. After a recent Sunday morning service, a new believer hurried up to report she had brought 18 people to church that day! She and her friends were working to fill a whole row across the auditorium. No one in her church had suggested that to her or her friends. It was the natural response of joy that stirred such enthusiasm. God's Spirit was moving their hearts and working through their faith to impact others for Christ.

Our new spiritual freedom moves us to share our faith.

Another motive for sharing one's faith grows out of a sense of indebtedness. We owe so much to God. We don't deserve to have our sins removed and forgiven. In the freedom God gives us from our sins there springs a new sense of obligation to obey and please Him. We are not deserving of the grace and mercy He so generously imparts. A growing faith learns to pray, "Lord, please don't give me what I deserve, but what I need." Now the previous fear of being in His presence is gone. His acceptance reminds us we are truly fortunate people. This sense of gratitude is often expressed with statements such as "God is so good to me" and "I'm so blessed." With the load of guilt and sin removed, we naturally want to help others make the same discovery.

A new sense of responsibility also motivates us.

We are also motivated to witness out of a desire to protect people from the natural consequences of their sins. We know heartache and sorrow will come unless they take the steps to change their lives with God's help. In one of the church families I minister to, a sister had begun to take drugs, neglect her family, and get in trouble with law enforcement. The family warned her. They pleaded with her. They asked her to reevaluate her life and her decisions. But she was convinced her way was an acceptable alternative. Eventually she reaped the consequences of her actions. Year after year, as she sat confined in her prison quarters, her family prayed for her to sense God speaking to her. They prayed God would give her the willingness to change her life's direction. They interceded God to bring someone into her life who would encourage her and direct her.

**We know
what is
coming . . .**

The family stayed in touch. They faithfully talked about the love of God. They didn't preach or condemn. But their persistence in caring and reaching out gave testimony to their desire to spare her from the painful and dangerous consequences of her wrong choices.

The inner desire to witness also comes from simply wanting people to experience dynamic and happy lives. That's the way it was for Sid. Sid had a wonderful Christian friend. They would laugh together, swap stories, and go hunting and fishing. They could entertain themselves simply by being together. Sid's friend wanted him to fully experience God's love in his life. The two had often talked about God, not because Sid was a horrible sinner, but because his believer friend wanted to see him free from some of his inner anxiety. He also hoped the anger that churned within Sid could find some resolution in light of God's unswerving love for him. Sid's friend really just wanted Sid's life to be better.

We love to be the first to share good news.

Another motivating influence within the human spirit that leads us to share our faith is an interest in seeing more believers in our fellowship. God has made us to be social creatures. We enjoy serving God among other people and take pleasure in worshiping God together. Bible study and prayer are more meaningful when others are included. When we tackle important tasks for God's sake, we like to do so in a group.

Good news just has to be told!

The Bible describes witnessing as sharing "good news." Have you ever found out some good news but were asked to keep it a secret? That can be very difficult, especially when the people we're with would love to know what we've discovered. If you've ever found a great bargain, you probably started telling your friends and family about it. We want to tell as many people as we can when we possess good news.

That's at least a part of the motivation in sharing our faith. We can hardly keep genuine faith to ourselves! We want everyone we care about to know the Lord too. Good news just *has* to be told.

This desire was evident when Richard, Jan, and their pastor were talking about starting a new church. The service time was directed toward people who were usually working on Sunday. They had friends and acquaintances who were also required to be working on Sunday mornings when most church worship services were usually held. "I think this church can be bigger than what any of us realize," Jan said. "I know lots of people who would come if we provided an alternative worship time. I'd love to see my family and friends worship with us."

Our core values stir us to share faith.

The desire to pass on our values to others is an important factor in why people witness. Truths we hold dear to our hearts cause us to communicate those values to other people. We want others to embrace the timeless principles in the Bible that we have found to be successful. Those principles, we believe, make up truth.

Christians have a set of values they have adopted, standards that Christ has given to us. For the Christian who is in love with Christ, the immediate interest is that others learn to love Christ and serve Him by adopting the same value system. This urge can become so strong that sometimes conflicts can result. Dissension can arise over what lifestyle is appropriate, what financial expenditure is wise, or even what kind of employment and career should be pursued.

Because the conflict can be so intense over the question of values, we fail to see that the difference in opinion can be an opportunity to give a winsome witness about Christ. Conflict is almost always an open door for witness, for the crisis becomes an opportunity to let love prevail. Jesus gave us two guidelines when facing situations where values conflict: *love your enemy* and *go the second mile*. Both of these spiritual insights address the Christian's attitude and response. We begin to understand it's more important to win a person to Christ than win an argument. We remember how long we resisted God's truth. As we keep our attitudes and actions Christlike and loving, our faith will be contagious. God's Spirit can melt the hardest heart and break through seemingly impossible barriers. As we are faithful to be Christ's representatives, the Holy Spirit will eventually penetrate the most difficult spiritual obstacles.

Christlike attitudes and actions are contagious.

Believers experience renewed joy when winning others.

The human longing for joy stirs a person to witness. The Christian's pursuit of joy, as recorded in 1 John 1:4, is in sharing what he or she has seen, heard, and experienced with God. A Christian longs to explain what God is really like. A primary reason for this is "to make our joy complete." Joy would not become full-blown if it were not for the opportunity to witness. Nothing brings spiritual renewal or a restoration of joy like winning others to Christ. If the truth about a great, gracious, and loving God

were not shared, joy would be smothered. As all our human ca-
pacity to rejoice enters into this celebration of new life, we must
tell others about God.

God can use the weakest efforts for sharing faith. Most Christians say that bringing someone to Christ is one of the greatest satisfactions
of their lives. We recall the first occasion of
personally leading someone to the Lord. Perhaps we were just teenagers, with more enthusiasm for witnessing than preparation or
training. But God can use the weakest efforts
for sharing faith. We never forget the exhilara-
tion of that moment. Since that day, we continually long to experience the deep delight of being used by God to see persons changed.

Subsequent encounters may not always be as sensational as
that first experience of leading a person to Christ. But we continue to grow in a deepening awareness of the pleasure in knowing
that heaven has touched earth—a person has met God and embraced His love.

We find joy in sharing the Good News regardless of the immediate result. Not all persons will respond positively and accept Christ at the time we ask them to. Although our response to
these occasions is not nearly as exhilarating, the awareness of being used by God, of obeying Him, of being a small portion of His
grand scheme gives us a quiet sense of joy that we have been
participants in a later harvest.

New believers share faith in their own relationships.

How is it that new Christians tend to witness more often
and more effectively than established Christians? New believers
are often caught up in the enthusiasm of their relationship with
Christ. The Bible is fresh to them. Prayer is so new and meaningful. The guilt that once possessed them is gone. They feel free.
Their new experiences become a source of conversation, delight,
and affirmation of their self-worth. They are convinced God has
done something special in them.

The new Christian prioritizes caring relationships over a
forced kind of witnessing. Friendships that have been nurtured
over the years among unbelievers are now exposed to a vibrant,
new Christian. The new believer simply explains what he or she

has experienced. He or she probably doesn't think in terms of *having* to witness; proclaiming the Good News comes out of the overflow of true-life experience. The new believer rejoices in what God has done, and he or she wants others to know about it.

Heartfelt enthusiasm can be very persuasive. Obligatory witnessing, the kind of witnessing that results from being pressured to share one's faith, is not nearly as interesting, intriguing, or inviting as the fresh, vibrant testimony of a new Christian. A real, heartfelt enthusiasm can be very persuasive.

The established Christian normally doesn't have as many close friendships with unchurched people as a new Christian does. The longtime Christian has generally gathered around himself or herself people who are also believers. It's just a natural phenomenon that such a fellowship forms. The established Christian will need to intentionally cultivate friendships and relationships with unbelievers. Most of us, after being in church for a number of years, find we must make the effort to build bridges to the undecided and unconvinced if we're to reach them for the Lord. In the present culture, most often we need to *earn* the right to share our faith with others. To have the greatest impact, a genuine friendship must first be cultivated and developed.

The new Christian has not experienced the persecution that so often shapes the outlook of an established Christian. Persecution hurts. Some Christians opt to avoid the pain and feared social rejection and to seek comfort and safety instead. Unfortunately, the result may be that spiritual influencing and faith shaping are no longer a part of their Christian experience.

Jesus spent considerable time preparing His disciples for persecution, warning them it was inevitable. He told them how to behave in light of persecution: keep loving people anyway, don't be deterred from your task of witnessing, and count it a privilege to suffer for God's sake. We need the same reminders today when social influence silences us so that we hesitate to tell what we have heard, seen, and experienced.

Sharing faith is more effective from the heart.

Too many believe sharing and shaping faith is more a head factor than a heart factor. I believe one of the reasons new Christians tend to witness more often and more effectively is that they have not been trained prematurely. Training that happens too soon can actually inhibit witnessing, because the new Christian then thinks there's a right and a wrong way to witness. He or she becomes more concerned with content than with relationships and learns *what to say* rather than how to become a spiritual adviser on an ongoing basis.

Jesus trained His disciples in everyday living. He simply modeled how a person shares his or her faith in a variety of circumstances. He sent His disciples out in groups of two to preach the Good News. After they came back, He then taught them what they did right and made corrections in their thinking. Educators call this approach the "action-reflection model" of learning. A person first acts out the behavior and then evaluates how it can be improved.

We witness out of love for God and other people.

Christians need training, but it would be well to approach training later on in the Christian experience. Training can be done as various circumstances arise, when questions are raised, when difficult encounters are reported. We're always to remember that we witness because we love God and people. Love speaks to the relational dimension of our lives. Witnessing shows how we care for people. Right words and proper theology will follow.

God has put within the heart of every Christian the desire to pass on to others the availability of a God-human relationship. They are then compelled deep from within to pursue that calling and to make that effort to talk to others about Christ. Meanwhile, God has placed within the heart of the unbeliever a desire for Him. Within the heart of every pre-Christian are found openness, receptivity, and longings. God then enables the Christian to follow an inner prompting to awaken that need. We can share the experience of the great Christian Paul, who wrote, "God did not give us a spirit of timidity, but a spirit of power, of love and of self-discipline" (2 Tim. 1:7).

5

How to Get Started Talking About God

. . . capture those particles of grace which act redemptively in a person's life, tiny vignettes that suggest God's work in a life. "How has God been at work in this person's life?"
—Ben Campbell Johnson
Speaking of God

Lyle

When I was a teenager, I was trained by both Campus Crusade and the Church of the Nazarene to use the *Four Spiritual Laws*, a booklet explaining how one receives Jesus Christ as personal Savior. We were sent out on the streets with the pamphlets to go door to door. At one home a man in his middle 40s responded to my knock. After talking with him briefly, I asked if he had heard of the *Four Spiritual Laws*. He responded that he had not, at which time I launched into the explanation of how God loved him and had a wonderful plan for his life. After a few minutes' explanation, I asked him if he would like to receive Christ into his life. He told me he had already done that 25 years before. He was a Baptist minister.

He obviously sensed my embarrassment and complimented me on my explanation of the gospel. He then asked me when the *Four Spiritual Laws* had been published, because he had not heard of them.

Even as a teenager who was not inclined to reflection, I realized that something was awry in my approach to evangelism. What was wrong? I had not taken enough time, or even made the effort, to find out where this Baptist minister was spiritually.

My assumption was a negative and judgmental one—that he was a sinner. The one question I did ask him, "Have you heard of the *Four Spiritual Laws*?" did not tell me anything more than that he had not heard the gospel packaged in this particular form.

The Christian must begin by hearing the pre-Christian. To be an effective witness, the Christian must begin the relationship with the pre-Christian by hearing carefully. Listen to discover where God is already at work in the person's life. God may have already been dealing with this person about spiritual matters. Perhaps he or she has a growing awareness of a need to be right with God or has a question about the Bible, the church, and spiritual things.

Joanie and her husband were questioning me as I sat with them around the fireplace in their living room. "Why are there so many different churches?" Joanie asked. "And where do the Mormons fit in? I have all these questions. In fact, I have so many questions I need to write them down when I think about them. I really don't understand if there is a God. And I'm always wondering why some things happen. I can't understand how God would allow some of the awful tragedies I read about to take place."

After attempting to answer some of her questions, I soon gave up—not because there are no answers to those questions, but because I discovered Joanie really didn't want to hear answers. She was most satisfied when I simply responded, "I'm pleased you're interested in spiritual things. Your questions and concerns tell me you have a spiritual sensitivity—you're attempting to respond to God, who's at work in your life."

"You know," Joanie said, "I do think a lot about God, although I'm not always sure He exists."

At this point I was again tempted to try to explain why a belief in God was reasonable, valuable, and important. If I had responded that way, I would have missed where Joanie was in the process of growing to faith. She wasn't ready to make a decision.

"Joanie, I'm excited about your spiritual interest. I hope you'll continue to see how God is at work in your life, to raise important questions, and to grab hold of the truth to which God guides you."

Discern the points of openness in the life of the pre-Christian. The opportunities to talk to people about Christ are not always obvious. Conversations start and stop, hesitate and start over, make detours, sometimes drift off course. The Christian who engages in intentional evangelism will continue to probe and inquire. Genuine interest in the pre-Christian gives us opportunities to direct conversations to spiritual things.

Many unsaved people express genuine concern about the future of the world, generally viewing it with some gloom and pessimism. This concern provides open doors for the ready witness. One option is to agree with the dire prediction. "As long as people leave God out of their lives, I don't have much hope for them," we could say. "Selfishness invariably leads to the disintegration of one's own life and society."

That may be too heavy a response for some Christians to give. Here's another possibility: "I'm optimistic about the future. I don't think God has ever let the world get out of control. A good, loving, and personal God has promised to take care of us—no matter what happens."

A third option might be, "It *is* easy to lose hope when we listen to the news—a tragedy every day. I just keep trusting God to direct me and my family. As a matter of practice, I've attempted to focus my attention on God's power rather than on the world's condition. It sure makes me feel better to look at life this way."

A spiritual guide is a companion who accompanies people on a spiritual journey.

Perhaps it would be well to think through what it means to be a spiritual guide. Our model for witnessing is often likened to a salesman or a preacher. At other times, we imagine that to be a witness we must be an expert on matters of the Bible and theology. The pre-Christian often thinks of the Christian as a judge. None of those roles are satisfactory for the spiritual director. A spiritual guide is a companion who accompanies people on a spiritual journey.

Even the New Testament imagery of the *shepherd* may not be as acceptable in our time because of its agricultural roots and the idea of herding people. The contemporary Christian can see the work of a shepherd as leading, rather than herding. A shepherd takes the journey before the sheep. But a shepherd is also mindful of those who struggle and works patiently to bring them along. With this understanding, the picture of a shepherd as a spiritual guide has value for the contemporary Christian.

"Spiritual adviser" may be too strong a term for some to feel comfortable with, for people are not altogether seeking advice. They want someone who will join them in the journey.

A *spiritual guide* is one who brings people into spiritual conversations, regardless of where those people are spiritually. In one sense, it's not important to ask, "Is this person right with God?" for the spiritual guide is one who is attempting to help anyone, saint or sinner, to move closer to God.

As Christians interested in sharing our faith, as spiritual guides, we find it helpful to have at hand some conversation starters. The following are merely suggestions that enable conversations to begin. Some of them may be more comfortable for you to ask than others. Create your own. The idea is to begin talking about God.

1. Do you give much thought to God and spiritual things?
2. Tell me about your most memorable spiritual experience.
3. What do you think is a person's greatest spiritual need?
4. Tell me about your church background; did you go to church as a child?
    a. How do you feel about your upbringing and your awareness of spiritual things?
    b. How would you describe your life with God now?
5. How do you think a person begins a personal relationship with God?
6. When did you feel closest to God?
    a. What were the factors or influences that brought you near God?
    b. What would renew that sense of closeness?
7. On a scale of 1-10 (10 being closest to God), where do you see yourself in relationship with God?
    a. Where do you want to be?
    b. How do you see yourself moving closer to God?
    c. How can I encourage you to get to where you would like to be?

The spiritual conversation starters allow you to easily introduce a spiritual topic into the conversation. Simply select a question or questions that tie into the former conversation or topics of interest. Some of the questions can be used in sequence. Proceed as long as your friend shows interest. Stay sensitive to his or her responses. Affirm any amount of truth or insight offered.

Listen closely. As we listen, several processes are taking place simultaneously in our minds. We generally organize what we hear in order to retain it. As I'm listening to someone talk, I listen for mention of his or her church background. This helps me identify how he or she views life.

I also listen to hear the theology reflected in their conversation. People usually express what they believe and don't believe about God. They will speak of excellent church experiences or woeful ones. As the pre-Christian talks, we Christians must be listening closely and organizing what he or she says into helpful categories in order to continue effective and meaningful communication.

As we're listening, we also make associations. That is, we connect what they're saying with various ideas, former experiences, or individuals we know personally. Another way association takes place is by translating words into meaning. We don't always understand the meaning that some people intend, because their words communicate something else to us. At these times it's important to repeat back to a person what you think he or she is trying to say, in order to ensure mutual understanding.

Another form of association is the connection between the speaker's facial expression and body language. If the meaning we attribute to the speaker's words does not jive with the expression or body language, we should clarify. We might ask, for example, "Are you feeling [scared, misunderstood, uncomfortable]?"

The process of interpreting words into meaning is going on simultaneously as the other person is speaking. Because we're able to think quicker than people speak, we're able to sort through the words, inflections, accents, and body language to bring about a reasonable approximation of what is meant.

We then attribute certain value to the information we hear. Sometimes we simply discard information; at other times we try to collect it. If we're trying to collect information, we generally will repeat it, or imagine some mental image, in order to come back and recall what we've heard.

The Christian witness must understand the person who's hearing the gospel presented is doing precisely the same sorts of mental evaluating, which we call listening.

Questions are not always objections to the gospel. That's another reason to make sure he or she understands. It's easy to consider another person's questions as objections to hearing the gospel, but they could be legitimate concerns or reflect a genuine interest in learning. Some methods of presenting the gospel are simply a means of staying in control of conversations. Effective witnessing will allow the pre-Christian to control how much information is given, how the information is given, and whether or not the gospel is received.

As we witness, we should be careful to express awareness through questions, feedback, and clarifications.

A benefit of listening, and listening attentively, is the ability to discern the obstacles preventing the pre-Christian from embracing God. The reason for discerning the obstacles is twofold: (1) the spiritual guide is able to see the barrier and enable the pre-Christian to address the primary issue; (2) the discernible obstacle may actually become the opportunity for dealing with the pre-Christian. As obstacles are removed, the human heart opens itself to God. If we ignore the obstacle, it continues to block the fulfillment of the human desire to be close to God.

Christians have long recognized one of the key obstacles in a person coming to Christ is self-sufficiency or indifference. The Bible talks about this obstacle by naming it "pride." A person appears not to be interested. After all, life is going well for him or her.

Childlike dependency is an expression of openness to God. I've discussed spiritual matters with people over the years who responded along these lines: "I don't feel I need God. Things are going fine right now." In other words, these people felt they were coping and successful quite apart from God. They concluded, until there was a reason to do otherwise, they would count on themselves and their resources to sustain them. In the Bible, Jesus warned rich and successful people about this very matter, saying that it was nearly impossible for a rich person to enter into the kingdom of God. Self-sufficient people resist a childlike dependency upon God.

A second obstacle that keeps people from entering into a saving relationship with God is extreme feelings of inadequacy or worthlessness, which are just the opposite of self-sufficiency. We're not to confuse these feelings with true guilt. Feelings of worthlessness are an expression of shame. Such people pack around feelings of self-hatred. They often battle thoughts of suicide. It's very difficult for them to actually believe God loves them. Sometimes these people have experienced terrible trauma, such as child abuse. They feel God has already abandoned them, so they're convinced He would have no desire to save them.

A third obstacle preventing a person from coming to God is an inward-directed anger. People feel they're too evil to be forgiven. They say things like "If you only knew what my past was" or "God can't forgive me." This is not a passing comment. The spiritual adviser should ask more questions rather than quickly reassuring them that God loves them no matter what. These feelings of anger are often accompanied with depression and extreme self-pity. They somehow feel they deserve punishment and that God is deriving pleasure from their suffering.

A fourth obstacle to people coming to God is they really don't understand Him. They are misguided people. Listening to their conversation, we will discover they have wrong concepts about God. They may see Him as punitive, outdated, and manipulative. They don't have the same word pictures in their minds that most Christians hold. The Christian sees God as light, as a dear Father, as a rescuer, as the Bread of Life. The unbeliever may see God as a crutch, a judge, and an executioner.

These misguided people have wrong information not only about God but also about the church. They have idealized the church to the point at which normal human people can't attend there without being hypocrites. At other times they'll see the church as simply money-mongers who want to take their hard-earned resources. They talk about the church as though it's impotent and inept. They don't see it as having any power or ability to help; they imagine it bumbles along as an ineffective organization. And while their stereotypes may not be altogether inaccurate, they fail to see the spiritual dimension, the pastoral care, and the value of the community of united believers walking through life together.

Wrong ideas about God and the church may be just the opening we need to pursue spiritual conversation and to challenge inadequacies in the pre-Christian's life.

A fifth obstacle preventing a person from relating to God is a strong will that insists on its own way. Self-made people are accustomed to living life on their own. They have pursued their own preferences rather than desiring and following after God's will.

A positive statement may bridge human effort to divine grace.

Once more, this obstacle can become an opportunity for the Christian witness. We can probe into the pre-Christian's conscience and consciousness by making statements along these lines: "You have a good mind, and you're a determined person. Obviously God has gifted you and provided resources for you to be successful. I imagine you're very appreciative." Such an affirmation of the person's ability and an acknowledgement of God's generosity toward him or her poses a proper understanding of the human situation. Such a positive statement bridges human effort to divine grace.

Another example of bridging between the self-made person and spiritual matters can be seen in this question: "With your strengths and abilities, you must have had the advantage of some wonderful people in your life. Who are the people God has placed along your pathway?"

The obstacles to faith are different for every unbeliever. Regardless of the specific issues, the question to address is "How do you envision life to be different if God were more of a part of you?" Even the saint can be asked that question. Each of us can envision God being more a part of our lives, although the pre-Christian may not have given much thought to such an inquiry.

The work of the Christian witness is likened to a wedge—gently separating a person from a wrong understanding of God so the Spirit might work to make God attractive. God could certainly have chosen to bring about conversion in each of us without using other people. But He chose not to. He intended to include us in His redemptive plan. Christians must learn to outthink and outlove the world. We must be willing to break the "sound barrier" by speaking up. When one effort is not successful, we're to learn from our failure. We're to try to develop new scripts the Holy Spirit can use in the hearts and minds of good but ungodly people. God wants to use you. He believes in you. He knows there will be some people who will not hear the gospel until you have pronounced good news in their hearing.

6

How Do We Pray for Someone?

Eph. 6:19-20

"Talking to men for God is a great thing," declared E. M. Bounds, "but talking to God for men is greater still." Intercession is placing emphasis on others rather than pleading for ourselves.
—Dick Eastman
No Easy Road

Lyle

A series of events led Sam further and deeper into sin. As a teenager, he became enraged because some guy at a club danced with his girlfriend. He grabbed a beer bottle, broke it, and with the sharp, jagged bottleneck, slashed the face of his adversary. Sam was a big six-foot-five-inch bruiser who enjoyed intimidating and humiliating people. It seemed he married just to divorce, going through women one right after another. Lying, stealing, and cheating were a way of life for him. He appeared to have no conscience or sense of moral conviction at all.

Day after day, week after week, year after year, Sam's brother, Elliot, prayed for him. Repeatedly and without remorse, Sam cheated Elliot, ridiculed him, and treated him unkindly. But Elliot prayed without ceasing until one day the jangling telephone suggested hopeful tidings. "I'm in the hospital," came the familiar voice when Elliot picked up the receiver. "I want Christ to save me."

Have you prayed for someone you love and care about and, as the years rolled by, wondered whether he or she would ever respond to God's call and come to know Christ as personal Savior? Perhaps you questioned whether it did any good at all to pray for that person.

We know the Bible teaches both prayer and evangelism as the Christian's privilege and obligation, but the temptation is to be discouraged when we see no results. It's not easy to persist in any activity that seems fruitless. Still, we know there's a definite relationship between prayer and the work of God's Spirit in bringing a person into a relationship with God.

There's a definite relationship between prayer and the work of God's Spirit in the life of a pre-Christian.

My wife, Paula, was introduced to Summer, a new Christian who was struggling to know how to live a Christian life with a husband who had no appreciation for her new "religion." He wasn't angry, but neither was he enamored. Paula found the following ideas helpful as she ministered to Summer and Roy.

1. Use a prayer list.

One day in Paula's quiet time with God, her devotional guide suggested developing a "ten most wanted" prayer list of unsaved people. "What a great idea!" she thought. She started her list with Roy, Summer's unsaved husband, at the top. She carried the prayer list in her Bible and prayed for Roy. To encourage Summer, she told her again and again, "Roy's at the top of my list."

For more then seven years Paula prayed for Roy, and also for Summer, that her life would be a testimony to him.

We invited Roy over to our house. After all, Paula was praying, we reasoned, so we might be able to develop a friendship there. They had children the age of ours. On occasion Roy would come to dinner with us or join us to view sporting events on television. Paula's prayers continued, "Lord, help Roy to become the Christian husband and dad his family needs. And don't let him give Summer a bad time. May he continue to be supportive of her church attendance and voluntary Christian service."

Upon seeing Paula at church, Summer would jokingly say, "Is he still on the top of your list?" After a particularly rough week, Summer would inquire, "Are you still praying for him?"

Roy would attend church occasionally, particularly when his

son was involved in the music. On Thanksgiving Family Sunday he joined his family and entered into the celebration. The year we left that church, Roy was saved. Today he's active in the Sunday School, serves on the board, and rarely misses worship services.

2. Pray for the person ministering to the unsaved.

Intercession, praying on behalf of another's salvation, is encouraged in Scripture. However, the Bible says more about praying for the Christian who is witnessing than praying for the unbeliever's salvation. The majority of prayers referenced in scripture focus on the believer's influence rather than on the pre-Christian's needy spiritual condition.

The apostle Paul prioritized those concerns when he wrote, "Pray also for me, that whenever I open my mouth, words may be given me so that I will fearlessly make known the mystery of the gospel" (Eph. 6:19).

Paul? With his dominant, aggressive nature, his articulate oratory, his fine spiritual training, how could he need to request prayer so he might talk to people about Jesus? As we read his New Testament letters, words seemed to flow easily for him. His thoughts were deep and penetrating and even mysterious. With his grasp of knowledge, his spiritual insight and fluency in language, surely he could have chosen his words well. His struggle was the same one you and I have: "That I may declare it . . . as I should" (v. 20).

Paul knew the mystery of the gospel could not be easily revealed to unbelievers. Today, false teachings and wrong impressions further cloud the path to understanding. It is easy to see why unbelievers have a hard time finding Christianity relevant to them. "Jesus Christ died 2,000 years ago," they think. "A Jew in a foreign land—dying for Americans who are not desperate? Somehow His death makes a difference in God's eyes, so the sins I commit here can be forgiven by a man who died 2,000 years before I lived? Isn't that mysterious? How can this be relevant to me?"

Our task is to make the gospel clear . . .

So our task is indeed a difficult one—to make the gospel clear when so much of it is strange to the ordinary person. We too ask, "How do I bridge the gulf between another person and myself; how can I introduce spiritual things?" This is a concern even if we are well-acquainted with the one to whom we speak.

3. Pray that the person ministering will have clarity of thought.

I have opened my mouth in certain circumstances and stuck in my foot, shoe included. I have regretted instances when my words should have been appealing rather than repelling. At those times I needed people to be praying for me so what I spoke would communicate what I intended.

Unlike us, Paul had reason to be fearful. Even as he wrote to the Ephesian church, he was in chains, having been thrown into prison for speaking truth about the Lord Jesus Christ. Few of us carry a long history of persecution for having propagated the gospel. But that doesn't keep our imaginations from running wild and being chased by our emotions. And we're so frightened that fear takes over and we find ourselves speechless. Paul needed prayer, and so do we.

4. Pray that the person ministering becomes bold.

A sense of "oughtness" compels us all, as believers, to tell our acquaintances, friends, and relatives what Jesus has done for us and wants to do for them. Although there are times when we would like to excuse, intellectualize, or talk our way out of the necessity to witness about Christ, there's always that prevailing inner "I should." Unfortunately, it's too often superseded by "I can't." This is not an *ought* we should discard, but a duty we should embrace—a step of faith we're obliged to take.

5. Pray for opportunities to witness.

Opportunities to witness don't automatically present themselves when we decide to take that step. We must pray for open doors. Paul said, "Devote yourselves to prayer, being watchful and thankful. And pray for us, too, that God may open a door for our message, so that we may proclaim the mystery of Christ, for which I am in chains" (Col. 4:2-3). Such devotion to prayer requires disciplined commitment.

My personal experience is that the more I pray, desiring opportunity, the more doors God opens. When I neglect to pray,
I'm apt to walk down the hallways of life unaware that doors are
ajar.

6. Pray for the ministering person to be accepting.

Paul's prayer includes the request for a proper presentation
of the gospel, without offense to the unbeliever: "Pray that I may
proclaim it clearly, as I should" (Col. 4:4), and the advice "Be
wise in the way you act toward outsiders; make the most of
every opportunity. Let your conversation be always full of grace,
seasoned with salt, so that you may know how to answer everyone" (vv. 5-6).

7. Use humor as a tool.

A sprinkling of humor also helps put your listener at ease. I
learned this through experience. I sensed some persons were ill
at ease as I presented the truth, not because I was doing anything
particularly wrong, but because they perceived me as unap-
proachable. The strategy I have used is to relate an experience
that makes me the object of my own joke, referring perhaps to
some stupid mistake I made. After sharing such an incident, one
friend had a good laugh at my expense and said, "That's so funny. I saw you as a totally together person who never made mis-
takes." Now we were on level ground. I was inviting this person
into a relationship with me. Paul's suggestion in Col. 4:6, that
our conversation be seasoned with salt, could include a sprinkling of humor to set the tone for the gospel presentation.

8. Guard your lifestyle and actions so to be a worthy witness.

How embarrassed I've been, again and again, by reports
from unbelievers about the clumsy, unwise attempts of Christians who tried to introduce them to Christ! Though I feel people
criticize Christians more than is justified, I'm poignantly reminded of the necessity for wisdom "in the way you act toward outsiders" (Col. 4:5). The too-casual approach, the careless word, the
temporary relinquishing of ethics, the unguarded lie—all these
legitimize the unbeliever's conclusion: "There's no difference be-

tween you and me. I don't see that you have anything to offer me."

9. Avoid judgmental comments.

When we think we have a right to be angry or disgusted with someone, let's relinquish that right for the more noble purpose of leading the unsaved into a right relationship with God. Sometimes when Christians think they are simply standing for principles, the outsider interprets their stand as perfectionism or judgmentalism. The door of opportunity is then slammed shut. Making the most of every opportunity means we guide a person, to the degree he or she is open, to a point closer to a right relationship with God. This requires tact and patience rather than coercion.

10. Don't pressure people.

Our approach must be loving and redemptive.

We must be careful not to quit before the opportunity has been fully exploited. Never are we to use high-pressure salesperson tactics. In conversation full of grace, we seize the opportunity God has presented, without patronizing. Our approach must be loving and redemptive, with a heart tuned to the welfare of others. Conversation "seasoned with salt" creates a thirst in the person to whom we're talking.

I carefully reasoned with Larry in my presentation of the gospel, leading him to a point of decision. I was disappointed when he responded, "In the last 30 seconds of my life I'll repent." I went home heavyhearted and told my wife, Paula. There in our living room we knelt and prayed for Larry. When we arose, I was astonished to learn we had prayed for an hour and 15 minutes. Though it had seemed only a few minutes, something had happened inside me during that time. I had a deep inner certainty that Larry would be saved. I can't explain such an experience, and it's not normal for me, but it was a certainty. Meanwhile, God's Spirit was at work in Larry's heart, creating hunger. Within two weeks he came to our home to report, "Lyle, I need you to know I've received Christ into my life."

11. Intervene positively in behalf of the pre-Christian.

Interceding really means intervening *positively* in behalf of a pre-Christian. Christians pray for unsaved people because sinners probably don't pray for themselves. God's Spirit nudges the Christian to pray positively for persons who cannot or will not initiate prayers. The positive intervention corrects such prayers as "Lord, wake him [or her] up at night! Make him [or her] miserable." If someone prayed for me that way, I'd prefer to recruit someone else to pray for me—someone who loved me!

Intercession imagines how God feels about the pre-Christian.

Genuine intercession imagines how God feels about the pre-Christian. Such praying asks for the eyes of God to see seekers as He sees them. Intercession captures the heart of God for the lost. We can't help but understand that how we pray determines how we treat the people we're trying to reach.

This kind of powerful praying includes a consecration of ourselves until God's heart and the heart of the praying person are united. There is a lingering in God's presence for an empathetic attitude, a persistence in faith until appropriate interaction with the pre-Christian is discerned.

Abraham's prayer intervention in behalf of Lot reflects both his trust in God and his love for a family member (Gen. 18:23-33). Intercession unites God's compassion with human concerns. Praying reveres God's power while regarding people's pitiful plight.

12. Begin now, and continue praying.

God's Spirit is working when we're asleep.

For some this arena of prayer and evangelism is unfamiliar. The important thing is to begin—now. The process may take not weeks, not months, maybe not even years, but decades. It's important to remember that the Spirit of God is working when we're asleep, and even when we've given up praying, He's still working.

God has called us to witness and to pray. That's a certainty.

Prayer registered in heaven is prayer dealt with by a God who is consumed with reaching perishing, lost people. He has chosen not to do it alone; He wants us to have the privilege of being His partner.

When you consider your need for empowerment as a witness, remember these prayer concerns:

- Introducing spiritual issues
- Making the gospel clear
- Praying to overcome fear
- Asking for open doors of opportunity
- Presenting the gospel winsomely
- Using a sense of humor

Praying for an unsaved person

1. First know you're in line with the will of God in your own life. Pray and search your heart.
2. Pray that you'll be able to show Christ to this person by your actions, words, and love.
3. Pray for patience, because it may be years before this person comes to know Christ.
4. Pray for the opportunity to be able to witness to this person.
5. Pray that God will send someone into the life of this person who will be the key to his or her coming to know Christ.
6. Ask God to speak to this person and to deal with his or her life.
7. Pray that God will soften the person's heart.
8. Pray for an obedient heart.
9. Pray that this person will be wise in the decisions he or she makes.
10. Pray that this person may know "how wide and long and high and deep is the love of Christ, and to know this love that surpasses knowledge" (Eph. 3:18-19).

11. Pray that this person will come to the point that he or she will hate sin.
12. Imagine this person discovering God at work.
13. Ask, "What about God, if it were known, would attract him [or her] to God?"
14. Ask, "How can I leak the good news about God?"
15. Pray that God's love will be experienced.
16. Pray that God's people will multiply loving words and actions.
17. Pray that God's people will become sensitive to the openness of people.
18. Pray that the ear of the unbeliever will be sensitive to the Holy Spirit's speaking.
19. Pray that the unbeliever will open his or her social circle to the Christian, and the Christian to the unsaved.
20. Pray that the unbeliever will see God at work in his or her life.
21. Pray that this person will reenvision God to be loving, just, good, and ultimately desirable.
22. Pray that this person will long for personal peace and freedom from guilt.
23. Pray that this person will desire to worship.
24. Ask, "What can I do or say today to bring Your light to his [or her] world?"

7

"I've Prayed—
Now What?"

Those who choose to follow Christ will eventually come to the conclusion that there's nothing more important than reaching people. . . . they're going to live differently, pray differently, love differently, work differently, give differently and serve differently, because they'll be preoccupied with people and their needs.
—Bill Hybels
Becoming a Contagious Christian

Jim

Every child needs a hero, and "C. J." was mine. As far back as I can remember, every summer included several weeks that I stayed with him and Mabel. They had no children and somewhat adopted me. I never knew a grandfather of my own, so I adopted C. J. for that role—and he was perfect for the part. One child's definition of grandfathers described C. J. so well: "Grandfathers are people who have time for kids." That was C. J.'s legacy in my life.

Cecil and Mabel lived in the small coal mining town of Wayland, Kentucky. She was a faithful member of the little church my father pastored. They tell me that it all began one Sunday after church when Mabel volunteered to take the preacher's baby home for the afternoon and bring him back to the Sunday evening service. (Now having been a father of two baby girls, I can certainly understand my parents' eager acceptance of that generous offer!)

Sunday afternoons soon expanded to other occasions, and this dear couple won a place in my heart. Somewhere in those blocks of time at Johnsons' house, they tell me, I learned to walk. In so many ways, C. J. made up for some of the inconveniences of being a "PK" (pastor's kid). He had the unique gift of making a child feel like the center of the universe.

I still remember our first tearful good-bye at five years of age. Our family moved from Wayland to Evansville, Indiana, for my father's new church assignment. C. J. brought me the gallon jar we had filled with all the marbles found on our evening walks. In my mind this good-bye was going to be forever.

You can imagine the excitement that next summer when the first of many annual bus tickets from C. J. arrived in my mailbox. I packed a little suitcase to spend several weeks at C. J.'s house. My father pinned a sign on my chest that read "Prestonsburg, Kentucky," sat me on the front seat of a Greyhound bus with my little suitcase, and shipped me off like a UPS package.

At the time, I couldn't understand why everyone who boarded the bus looked at me and began to laugh. The first few stops I smiled with their amusement. But by the end of the trip I was one very frustrated five-year-old! That was one of the longest trips of my life. But spying C. J. when those bus doors hissed open wide quickly erased my misery.

Each summer of my childhood included a bus trip to eastern Kentucky, but I insisted that dad put no more signs on my chest. The daily schedule at C. J.'s was great. I slept until I wanted to get up. Then I would fix my own pancakes from the batter he would leave me before he left to work in the mines. While Mabel did her household chores, I spent the morning watching cartoons and children's programs on television. Afternoons were spent exploring the creeks and looking for "pop bottles" for deposit returns.

I was always waiting on the back steps when the steam whistle blew at the mining temple, signaling the end of the shift. C. J. was covered in coal dust every day when he came home from work, so I had to wait for him to clean up. After that, we would go fishing—every evening!—always to a new spot where we knew the fish would be biting. After dark, the ride home included stopping by the town's only general store to tell a few fish stories and pick up my choice of a new pint of ice cream.

After supper we would take an evening walk, visiting with

all the neighbors, catching up on the news in the little town. Then home for the wrestling matches on television—and on the living room floor! Eventually we would wear down and eat our ice cream. In the late-night glow of the television set we would begin to doze off. Finally, each night we would climb up the narrow stairway to a contented summer sleep. All to be repeated again the next day.

I just couldn't imagine heaven without him . . .

Needless to say, those happy childhood memories of summer endeared Cecil Johnson to me. In my limited estimation, they didn't come any better. That's why I was stunned to learn that C. J. wasn't a Christian. He had never accepted Jesus into his heart. As a child, I just couldn't imagine heaven without him being there. My parents explained that we needed to pray for him so that one day he would become a Christian, which in childlike faith I began to do immediately.

As far back as I can remember, I included that request in every prayer, as a closing line just before "in Jesus' name. Amen." Even my sisters and brother picked up on the line, "and God, save C. J." in their bedtime prayers.

We took turns at our house for prayer for our meals. Since there were seven around our table, each member of our family had one day of the week to say the mealtime prayers. Friday was my day. So for breakfast and supper that day the line was always included "and God, save C. J. In Jesus' name. Amen."

The years went by, and all the summers of my childhood included the bus ride to Prestonsburg and Wayland, Kentucky. The annual treks ceased when our family moved to south Georgia, and there I entered high school. But later in college I began to plan my long drives to college to go through Wayland and see my surrogate grandparents. All through those years I continued to pray for this coal miner in eastern Kentucky to come to faith in Jesus Christ.

After I sensed the call of God into ministry and began training, one of my courses was on personal evangelism. Our professor infected us with a passion for winning others to Christ by learning how to dialogue about faith. Our final exam for the class was to memorize how to begin a conversation about spiritual things and then lead someone into a simple presentation of the gospel.

This was going to be the time all our prayers would be answered . . .

While my classmates worked for an "A" on the final exam, I drilled myself on the presentation for a more personal reason. After a sleepless week of final exams, I drove straight from the college campus to Wayland for "a dinner appointment" with C. J. All through our meal I waited for the right opportunity to bring up the subject, but it just didn't happen. I just knew after nearly 20 years of praying, this would be the night he would accept Christ. Tonight, all our prayers for C. J. would be answered!

Finally, on the ride back to C. J.'s house, I pulled the car over onto the side of the road, turned off the engine, and went for broke. After nervously stumbling through my best possible attempt for persuading him to become a Christian, C. J. quietly said, "You know, Jim, I've thought a lot about this. I do appreciate you sharing with me. But I'm just not ready yet." We closed our conversation in prayer together, and I asked God to help C. J. "to get ready in his life and to want to become a Christian."

On the 700-mile drive home, those words echoed in my ears. "I'm just not ready yet." To just say I was deeply disappointed would have been a gross understatement. If all those years of praying every day hadn't made him ready, what would? Why wouldn't he say yes to the best offer in his life?

I became frustrated with God. Hadn't He promised in the Isa. 55:11 (KJV), "My word . . . shall not return unto me void"? Didn't He tell us in Matt. 7:7 (KJV) to "ask, and it shall be given you"? There seemed to be nothing else I could do to win C. J. for the Lord. And it sure didn't seem to me the Lord was helping out in the situation either.

Divine delays can strengthen our faith.

What else could I do to bring him to faith? Have you ever been there? Have you ever felt like that?

When we read through the faith chapter in Heb. 11, we see that waiting and delays in the lives of the faithful occur with profound regularity. These divine delays seem to shape and strengthen faith. Abraham was 99 years old before he received his promised miracle child. Noah waited 120 years for rain. Nearly every promise in Joseph's life was delayed. The list of those who trusted God and were faithful without having their prayers answered could go on and on. The Heb. 11 passage closes with a reminder:

These were all commended for their faith, yet none of them received what had been promised. God had planned something better for us so that only together with us they would be made perfect.

While we all love the experience of the occasional miracle, the patient prayer is actually the faith builder. In the spiritual waiting rooms God teaches us to trust Him and persevere. We prefer the quick-fix miracle, but God works in us through the waiting. While He pushes the "pause" button in our lives, we would much rather "fast forward."

Most of us just hate to wait. Our culture conditions us to believe that waiting is always negative. It's an inconvenience, which is unpardonable in a consumer culture. We have microwave ovens, E-mail, overnight shipping, and satellite news. Slow service in a fast-food restaurant? That's nearly unbearable!

Waiting helps us see the eternal view. But God has a different perspective. Waiting melts our will in full surrender to His designs. In God's delays we begin to see through eyes of faith as His plan unfolds. Delays increase our dependence on Him. While we put things in a spiritual holding pattern, we have the opportunity to view life from the eternal perspective.

Sometimes in our consumer mentality, we view prayer like God's divine customer service line. We are the customer. God is the company. We place the order with God as we pray. Sometimes we even place a rush order for an overnight delivery. And then we expect an answer at our door the next morning. Waiting enables us to change that mind-set.

The Scriptures teach us that we're not the customer—we're the clay. God is not the company—He's the Potter. Prayer is not placing our personal order for God's service to us. Waiting in prayer becomes an act of placing ourselves in God's hands for serving Him and others as He sees fit. Waiting shapes our faith and molds us into the vessels of service for eternal significance.

Sometimes the waiting is for weeks or months. Sometimes we wait for years. The longer I prayed for C. J.'s salvation through those years, the more it seemed clear that it would only be a matter of time. God seemed to affirm it to me over and over—if I would be faithful, He would make our faith-sharing efforts fruitful.

Particular verses of promises became assurances that C. J. would come to faith:

Jesus told them a story showing that it was necessary for them to pray consistently and never quit (Luke 18:1, TM).

They that sow in tears shall reap in joy (Ps. 126:5, KJV).

We were really crushed and overwhelmed . . . and saw how powerless we were to help ourselves; but that was good, for then we put everything into the hands of God, who alone could save us, for he can even raise the dead. And he did help us . . . and we expect him to do it again and again (2 Cor. 1:8-10, TLB).

One verse that became God's promise to me for C. J. was Gal. 6:9, which I paraphrased, memorized, and prayed through regularly:

Don't get too tired in doing what God has called you to do. In His time you'll see the results you want to see if you don't quit (author's paraphrase).

The problem is not that some people are too difficult to reach for Christ. The real problem is that we just give up too soon. I began to persist in prayer even more for C. J.'s salvation.

So we kept the prayer going through those years. The Lord blessed our pastoral ministry in unusual ways in personal evangelism. Before graduating from college, I was carrying around a prayer list of more than 50 people we had personally introduced to Christ. As each new person came to know the Lord, my heart's prayer was "Now, Lord, send someone to C. J. for me."

The conviction grew that God would reward our faithfulness.

Each of my letters to Wayland would close with, "We're still praying for you." Without trying to confront C. J. incessantly and make faith an uncomfortable topic, we also lived in the tension of keeping the seeds of truth sown in his life. The conviction grew that God would reward our faithfulness in reaching the people around us by sending some faithful believer into C. J.'s life.

Several more years went by. One Monday morning I came into the church office to tackle the stack of mail and the usual mountain of details. After a few letters into the routine came a white card in an envelope from Wayland that read:

C. J. is very ill and last week was diagnosed with cancer. He is taking chemotherapy treatments now, and we ask that you pray for him. But he wanted me to write and tell you that last month before he went to the doctors, he went forward at a revival meeting and asked Jesus into his heart. He was baptized. He just thought you'd like to know.

Just thought I'd like to know! What an understatement! I hurried out of the church office to my secretary's desk and held up the card exclaiming, "C. J. got saved! Look at this—C. J. got saved!" She had no idea who I was talking about and said, "Oh, that's nice." I called my wife at her office and told her the news. Next I called my parents and finally placed a call to Wayland so we could celebrate together.

In a few days we made the trip back to the mountains of eastern Kentucky, down familiar roads and childhood's memory lane. Rhonda, my wife, and my father accompanied me back for this memorable reunion. When we walked into his living room, where his hospital bed had been placed, C. J. slowly got up from his bed. His first words to my father and me were "I've always called you Paul and Jim, but now you're my brothers!" We all embraced in a joyful huddle.

"Now you're my brothers!"

We visited for several hours and relived many happy memories. After an evening meal and final prayer together, we left for our responsibilities back home. Our next meeting was scheduled in two weeks, when I would take C. J. to the hospital in the next county for another treatment.

But the call came a few days after we arrived home.

I was asked to conduct the memorial service in the little church my father had pastored years before. My text was from Gal. 6:9 (KJV):

Let us not be weary in well doing: for in due season we shall reap, if we faint not.

We all have loved ones who need to come to faith in Christ. The burden we carry for them is from the Lord. We become the bridge from Him to them. With God's help and guidance, we can be the one to plant the seeds of faith in their lives. There are no instant harvests. But His Word is true:

Don't get too tired in doing what God has called you to do. In His time you'll see the results you want to see if you don't quit (Gal. 6:9, author's paraphrase).

God is faithful. His Word is powerful and alive. His truth will not change, even though we may be praying for years.

Don't get too tired. . . . in His time . . .

8

"Who Should I Talk To?"

When God purposes to do something through you, the assignment will have God-sized dimensions. This is because God wants to reveal Himself to you and to those around you. If you can do the work in your own strength, people will not come to know God. However, if God works through you to do only what He can do, you and those around you will come to know Him.

—Henry T. Blackaby
Experiencing God

Jim

There is a fascinating Bible story found in 2 Kings 6 and 7 that teaches us a great deal on the subject of sharing our faith. Enemy armies had encamped around Samaria and had laid siege to her population. The situation had become quite desperate for the inhabitants of the city, and graphic descriptions are given of their plight. While the enemy armies encircled the city, the people inside the city walls were slowly dying of starvation.

As the story unfolds, we are directed to four lepers living outside the city gates. They were forbidden by their countrymen to live within their city because of their physical illness and contagious condition. The lepers' situation seemed hopeless. They were outcasts even from their own fellow countrymen. They had no hope for recovery from their physical condition. The enemies of their country had them trapped and starving like the rest of the city.

The biblical story picks up with these four lepers having an intense conversation about their horrible condition. Eventually they conclude they have only these options:

Option 1: We can stay here and die of starvation, waiting for the end to come to us slowly where we are. The result is certain: If we do nothing, we're surely going to die.

Option 2: We could go back into the city and try to find nourishment, but the truth is that they have no more to eat in there than we have out here. The result? We'd starve—it would only be a matter of time.

Option 3: We could walk out to the campfires we see burning at night in the hills around us. We could beg the enemy soldiers there for food or scraps of leftovers. Maybe we could find someone to have pity on us and spare our lives.

As the lepers weighed this last option, the conversation may have gone something like this:

"The soldiers will kill us for bothering them. There's no real promise of any help—no hint of mercy out there." And then the King James Version quotes them as saying, "But if they kill us, we shall but die" (2 Kings 7:4).

"Option 3 isn't bright with promise, but it's really our only chance."

The cost of doing nothing was too great . . .

As many of us facing personal changes and risks would do, these four finally decide to go for it and make a change since the pain of the present and the bleak potential of doing nothing only invite the inevitable. The cost of doing nothing was too great not to make some kind of attempt at personal change.

The choices these four lepers faced are a lot like the decisions we must make when confronted with change. The humorous definition of insanity is "to do what we've always done, and then expect the results to be different!" Max Dupree said it even better: "We cannot become what we need to be by remaining what we are."

At some point we must take a survey of our lives in the honest light of day and say, "Based on what we can see and know and validate, something has to be addressed, and change has to happen." The same process happens in shaping our faith. To move up to new levels of trusting God, we make choices and decisions that require greater commitment.

This process occurs even in sharing our faith. We consider

[handwritten margin notes: "to miracle was in t. choice of timing by t. lepers to enter that certain day!"]

the commitments and responses needed to effectively impact the faith of others. We weigh the options and consider the costs involved with each choice. But too many times we don't really understand the facts.

A significant day of decision in United States history illustrates this principle. On June 25, 1876, General George Armstrong Custer received information that a number of Indians were gathering at Little Big Horn in the northern plains. Without fully investigating all the facts, he decided to ride out with 250 men to "surround" the group of rebellious Indians. But there was something he didn't know—the Indians numbered nearly 3,000. The results of his decision are known in history as "Custer's Last Stand."

The four lepers decided together to dare to change. As they considered their options and the results of each of those choices, they realized they had to risk the trip to the enemy's camp. But when they walked into the camp they made an incredible discovery: everyone was gone. The lepers couldn't have known that during the night the Lord had frightened all these enemies away with the sounds of a mighty attacking army. The enemies abandoned their camp, leaving everything behind—tents, food, drink, clothes, armor, and even treasures.

Suddenly it was like the world's largest smorgasbord. They found themselves surrounded by food—and all free! Imagine how these men must have felt. A sense of relief, then surprise, quickly turned to celebration. Picture how they must have acted, running excitedly through the camp gathering up everything they could eat or carry. They literally went from famine to feasting. They partied like never before. They went from desperation to celebration, from poverty to plenty, from being starved to being stuffed! They had a feast like they had never eaten in all their lives. Then like many who have gone through times of poverty, they started to hoard it up and hide all they could get their hands on. They began to dig holes to bury their newfound loot.

Suddenly one of the lepers spoke to the rest of the group: "Hey, guys, we can't do this. Look at our city, sitting in the dark down there. All those people are starving like we were. We've got more than enough here—there's no less for us if we share it."

They began to hurry back to the city. "Let's host an even bigger party," one must have said. "I've got to find my family and friends!" another shouted back. "I only hope I'm not too late!"

When the men arrived at the city they heralded the word through the streets: "Come and get it! All you can eat—free food! The siege is over! The enemies are gone!"

"Sharing your faith is just like one beggar telling another beggar where to find bread."

There's so much to learn from this wonderful story. These lepers bringing their townspeople out to the feast is a lot like what we read of the Early Church in the Book of Acts. Someone has said, "Sharing your faith is just like one beggar telling another beggar where to find bread."

When you read Acts 2, you find the same sense of excitement and joy.

They devoted themselves to the apostles' teaching and to the fellowship, to the breaking of bread and to prayer. . . . All the believers were together and had everything in common. . . . Every day they continued to meet together . . . And the Lord added to their number daily those who were being saved (Acts 2:42, 44, 46-47).

The story of the lepers outlines powerful principles for a group of believers to shape and share faith in the lives of others:

1. Caring grows from a sense of discovery.

We shape faith and share it out of our own personal experience. The lepers eventually turned their attention to their friends inside the city after their own needs were filled. When they realized they had more than enough for everyone, they hurried back to those they knew, to share what they had discovered. Believers who are most satisfied in their own faith—like the filled and satisfied lepers—are the ones who seem to focus their attention on others in need.

Personal satisfaction is a great motivator.

The pattern is repeated throughout the Scriptures. We begin with those we know the best. In more than one instance, Jesus instructed us to share the gospel with those who were most ready to receive the truth. Personal satisfaction is a great motivator.

Interestingly, while the lepers were

starving they made no mention of the rest of the hungry population. They were concerned only about their own misery. But after they had eaten their fill, the needs of others made them uncomfortable. There could be no real contentment if others were dying without hope, as they had been just a while ago.

2. Concern flows from a sense of responsibility.

Once we have discovered the source of help that has met our needs, it motivates us to get the good news to others we care about. We are like the lepers finding a camp full of food and supplies and hurrying back to their friends and family. When we discover the difference Jesus Christ can make in our lives, we also find a new sense of responsibility to share God's truth with others.

The apostle Paul described it like this: "God . . . reconciled us to himself through Christ and gave us the ministry of reconciliation" (2 Cor. 5:18).

Faith sharing is like leading starving people to food.

This picture of faith sharing is like leading starving people to food. Notice the difference in the two different trips the lepers made to the enemy's camps. The first time they went in fear and trembling, hungry and needy. They were intimidated by what they might face. Desperation about the future was all that moved them to go. They had little hope of finding any help. They went because they *had* to go.

The second trip out to the camp was much different. They had already eaten and were feeling stronger. They took their friends and family with them. The lepers were not filled with dread, but now with delight. The sense of intimidation had been replaced with anticipation of all the good things that were waiting to be discovered. They went because they *wanted* to go!

Many believers who desperately want to share their faith have attitudes that reflect the first trip to camp rather than the second. The Scriptures teach that "perfect love casteth out fear" (1 John 4:18, KJV). In a new spirit of expectancy, we can bring our loved ones to the place of spiritual celebration as together we discover all that God has in store for us. We want to share our faith with others—sharing not because we have to, but because we *want* to!

When we seriously consider the spiritual options for those without Christ, we cannot enjoy God's blessings without sharing the good news we have discovered. Because we know, we want to go and share with them.

3. Compassion shows in a sense of urgency.

We may not be able to help everyone, but we can reach someone.

Real compassion is reflected in our attitudes. Genuine love moves us to do something. Compassion flows from an individual's realization that the situation is desperate and that action must be taken. To do nothing is totally unacceptable. We may not be able to help everyone, but we can reach someone.

Can you imagine the intensity of the four lepers as they went back into the city to find their friends, neighbors, coworkers, family, and acquaintances? Do you think they would have casually accepted a "No, thank you" from someone they really cared about? Undoubtedly they had some energetic exchanges in order to convince certain people to accompany them out to their newfound discovery.

It's been my observation that few people ever come to faith in Christ until a believer somewhere has a sense of urgency about their spiritual need. As our prayer life deepens, we become increasingly moved about others who need to come to faith in Christ. Compassion becomes a lifestyle.

Jesus illustrated this truth so dramatically in Luke 15 by showing the need for a new sense of urgency if the lost are to be found. The shepherd leaves the 99 to go find the lost one. The woman won't sleep until she finds her missing coin. The father's attention is on the horizon as he searches for his wayward son to come home. Nothing was more pressing or urgent. It's as if Jesus is teaching the reason the lost are found is that someone somewhere feels a sense of urgency about their need!

The psalmist captured that sense when he wrote,

They that sow in tears shall reap in joy. He that goeth forth and weepeth, bearing precious seed, shall doubtless come again with rejoicing, bringing his sheaves with him (Ps. 126:5-6, KJV).

In God's redemptive plan for shaping faith, one of the components depends on believers who will become the link in the chain of faith, someone who will care enough to share. The kingdom of Christ is built by faith-filled and faithful Christians who will take the responsibility to win the spiritual seeker God brings into their lives. How long can you continue to hope and pray for someone who needs to come to faith in Christ?

A guiding principle for life is to get as many people to heaven as we possibly can!

If we could convince one person to come to the spiritual feast, would we stop there? No doubt the lepers began telling everyone they could after reaching those they knew. And then the web of relationships in the city began to engage—until everyone came to the celebration. We may begin with a few, but we can't ignore the masses. A guiding principle for life is to get as many people to heaven as we possibly can!

Nothing is as thrilling as someone responding positively to come to trust Christ. From the first invitation, to the most recent new believer, the joy continues.

4. Commitment knows a sense of intensity.

Shaping and sharing faith in others demands a commitment in my life. To effect change in others, change must begin in me. The pattern is found throughout the Bible, but very clearly here in the story of the lepers. As they considered their own needs and the options facing them, reality moved them into a life-changing decision. They dedicated themselves to telling everyone else in the city about their discovery.

If we become serious in sharing our faith, it means some things in our lives will change. Of course, we need to maintain a faithful lifestyle and be consistent in our words and actions. But greater influence demands greater intensity. At times we will defer our personal preferences for the spiritual needs of others. "We can't just keep this to ourselves," the lepers said. "We have to go back to the city and tell everyone else!"

When we become convinced of our task in reaching others for Christ, we begin to lay aside our interests for this priority.

When The Family Church began, we decided to plan our worship services with the seeker in mind. Together we purposed to give them the "best" seats—the ones in the back of our auditorium and closest to the doors. Our members and regular attendees park farthest away from the auditorium so the first-time attendees get the best parking places. As we plan our weekend services we keep the newest, most needy people in mind.

John Reed was one of my spiritual heroes. He modeled this principle of self-sacrifice in his life and served faithfully in one of the churches I pastored in the Midwest. I asked John one winter day about the old car he was driving. One door was wired shut, and the metal springs were showing through the seat covers. The heater was broken, and one window wouldn't close completely. In a teasing way, I asked him why he didn't get a real car. His answer will stay with me forever. He smiled and said, "Pastor, if I had to buy a new car, I couldn't keep my 23 missionary shares." I knew that meant he invested more than $200 every month to help support Kingdom building around the world through missionaries he had helped send. John had given up his personal preferences and comfort to intensify efforts in sharing faith.

That was the attitude and spirit modeled by the New Testament Church. 1 John 3:18 admonishes us, "Let us not love with words or tongue but with actions and in truth." Do you sense this spirit of intensity in Rom. 15:2? "We must bear the 'burden' of being considerate of the doubts and fears of others" (TLB). If people are to be reached, the accommodations must be made by us—not by them. That's a higher level of intensity. But our commitment yields incredible returns.

Intense faith sharing with others influences incredible faith shaping in our own lives. P. T. Forsyth said, "You must live with people to know their problems and live with God in order to help solve them." As we resolve to reach more people for Christ and increase our intensity level in faith sharing, God begins to bless our lives in new and multiple ways.

9

"How Should I Approach People?"

As Jesus walked beside the Sea of Galilee, he saw Simon and his brother Andrew casting a net into the lake, for they were fishermen. "Come, follow me," Jesus said, "and I will make you fishers of men." At once they left their nets and followed him.
—Mark 1:16-18

Lyle

Kevin had watched Christians and wondered if he should choose Christ. For two years he had dated a girl who was a wonderful example of Christian love and virtue. Her church attending parents also served as examples.

One day he listened to Bob, one of his coworkers, tell about an accident in which a man was swept downriver by the flood current. The endangered man swam and fought the raging water, but without success. Suddenly the river threw the swimmer into a narrow channel near an eroded bank. The man grabbed an exposed root and pulled himself to safety.

Bob simply concluded his story, "That guy can thank God that He provided something to hang onto."

Kevin, already thinking about accepting Christ, connected this story to the godly lives of his girlfriend and her folks. He came forward to pray at an altar two Sundays later.

Evangelism involves a process of decision-making on the part of the lost people. Pre-Christians probably have been influenced several ways before finally deciding to become a Christian.

Christians who effectively evangelize understand the decision-making process. In fact, the Christian who wants to influence the secularist must think as the unsaved person thinks. This change in thinking may require an expanded understanding of evangelism.

Evangelism encompasses more than the point of sharing faith.

Many of us consider evangelism to be the moment of witness when Christians share their faith in God and invite a sinner to receive Christ as Savior. That is indeed evangelism, of course, but it encompasses much more before and after the decision to invite God into one's life.

A study of how people come to know God indicates that there must be several positive exposures to the gospel before a person accepts Christ. Win Arn, a church growth consultant, noted that people who accept Christ and stay in the church heard the gospel an average of 5.7 times before they decided to serve God. Because we're anxious to see people converted, we're inclined to take shortcuts, to apply pressure, or to give up too soon. This is not the way Jesus worked. Successful witnessing continually communicates a winsome brand of Christianity while showing an interest in the unbeliever.

Research also shows more than one person is involved in the redemption process. God uses several people and usually over a significant period of time. After numerous people, several influences, and a half-dozen hearings of the gospel, a person chooses to become a disciple of Christ.

More than likely people who are evangelized will explore their relationships with God in much the same way they make decisions in other areas of their lives. For example, if a young adult decides to buy a car, he or she will ask some friends which models they like, which are durable, which give good gas mileage, and so on. The individual will then visit some dealerships whose reputations he or she has already investigated and will test-drive several cars. Finally, this person will make a purchase decision based upon his or her personal research.

People who are exploring a relationship with God will often visit several local "dealerships," that is, nearby churches or Bible studies. When spiritual seekers find some people with whom they are comfortable, they will then begin the actual decision-making process to move toward Christ, acknowledging their need for God. The search culminates in a prayer of faith to God. Newly found friends at church have served as one influence in bringing these people to God.

Thus, to be effective evangelistically, we must continue cultivating friendships, planting additional seeds, looking for opportunities to harvest. Some churches follow those processes very well. A few congregations press too hastily, resulting in premature decisions. Yet others are so fearful of harvesting prematurely that they never invite people into a relationship with God.

The church has an awesome challenge—to make disciples! Evangelism—the effective kind—must be done with sensitivity and intentionally. But it must be done. The church has no greater purpose than making disciples. Spiritual leaders need to recognize that evangelism involves a process. Let's discuss some of the components in that process.

Evangelistic effectiveness starts with the credible behavior of the Christian. A Christian's lifestyle establishes his credibility in the mind of the unbeliever. The witnessing Christian interacts lovingly with the observing unbeliever. When the unbeliever sees consistency between the witness and his message, the unbeliever often accepts the message of the witness. If the unbeliever doubts the authenticity of the witness, he will not be moved to accept either the message or the messenger.

Rita is a young woman who was greatly influenced by the compassionate ministry she saw in the Community of Hope church in Washington, D.C. Rita observed godly people restoring a building in her blighted neighborhood. She discovered in their activity an elevated self-esteem, hope, and help. Over time she began to explore a relationship with Christ.

Good deeds often make evangelism effective. The generous person who shares his or her resources will have an impact upon unbelievers. The person who visits an acquaintance in the hospital earns the right to speak of God. In fact, Jesus made it clear that our good works are a way by which we can help people see God (Matt. 5:16). The credible life of holiness opens a window so pre-Christians can envision God.

Effective evangelism requires increased friendships with unbeliev-

ers. The outsider is easily neglected when the vast majority of church work ministers only to people who are already part of the church. The congregation must intentionally find ways to intersect with unbelievers.

Jesus did that so well. He often spent time among people with questionable reputations and socially unacceptable behavior. One of the finest commentaries on His ability to interact with the world was that He was "a friend of tax collectors and 'sinners'"(Luke 7:34).

Mark, new at the tennis club, attempted to get to know Sid, one of the better players. Sid at first ignored Mark—refusing even to exchange hellos in the hallway. Sid's angry behavior and cheating on scores alienated him from most of the tennis players. Finally Mark was able to play against Sid, who won handily. Mark complimented him and asked for some helpful pointers. As a result, Sid began to chat with Mark.

Upon walking into a restaurant one weekend, Sid jumped to his feet, yelling across the busy establishment, "Hey, Mark—how are you doing?" Ignoring Sid's shouting in public, Mark walked to where Sid was seated, knowing he had won a friend and had built a bridge to Sid's heart.

Effective evangelism identifies the level of spiritual receptivity and works to help people become open to the gospel. Christians, because they have a great commitment to the Good News, are tempted to begin with the Good News and proclaim it without regard to the level of openness in the mind of the individual.

I was strolling along a creek bed with a handful of prayer requests that church people had shared with me, their pastor. I was praying for them when I noticed a man with a Volkswagen bus decorated with religious slogans. He was filling plastic milk jugs with water from the sulfur springs. I asked him what he did with the water. He told me of the great medicinal value he had discovered in the water. He then promptly diverted the conversation to my need for the Lord. For three to five minutes, nonstop, he told me how I should get saved. At the end of his monologue, he reached in his pocket, took out a tract, handed it to me, turned on his heels, and walked off. I was both amused and disgusted. Apparently this well-intentioned man had never even thought to determine where I was spiritually. He had only in mind to tell me what I "needed" to hear and what he wanted to say.

I confess I have made the same mistake by assuming people were not right with God. And while they may not have been right with God, they thought they were. I judged them because I had made some wrong assumptions. How much wiser to explore with people where they think they are spiritually.

Evangelism begins by listening to the language the other person speaks. *Evangelism includes constructive and accurate listening.* Evangelism begins with listening rather than proclamation. We must know the language the person speaks, the values he or she possesses, his or her understanding of God's work in his or her life, and his or her expectations of what being a Christian means.

A reasonable question for the soul winner is "How well do I listen?" God always deals with us where we are. Since we humans don't have all knowledge available to us, we must ask questions and listen intently to discover where people are and their measure of openness. This is not unlike God. That's how He treats us.

Evangelism involves speaking. We're to testify about what we've heard, seen, and experienced. This principle should alleviate some of the inner fears we experience about sharing our faith. Some Christians feel they must be able to answer all of another person's questions. But a witness is never expected to tell what he does *not* know. Christians are to describe what they know to be true from personal experience.

Since witnesses are to tell what they have seen, we would do well to increase our "God sightings." For example, we can learn to interpret our experiences in light of God's work and share that information with others.

I was speaking in a humanities class at a state college in the Midwest. Upon completion of the class, six or seven students crowded around the lectern to talk with me about God. One young man lingered after the rest had strolled away. As I started to leave the building, he walked with me. Finally he blurted out, "I just don't see God the way you do. You make Him sound likable. I guess the reason I've never really believed in God is that I've always thought of Him as negative and judgmental."

"Well, I would have a hard time believing in a God like you

describe too," I responded. "Although it may not answer all of a person's questions, my experience is that God is loving, kind, and fair. He wants the best for us."

In giving advice, we're painting a picture of what a person can become.

Evangelism requires that Christians become spiritual advisers. Evangelism is guiding as well as telling. When we understand where people are in their spiritual journey, then we can encourage them to take additional steps toward God. Spiritual advising consists of giving good news rather than bad news. A Christian has much more to say than to describe the bad habits from which he or she is free. Jesus brought good news. His message explained who He was and what He was like. As we give advice, we're painting a picture of what a person can become.

Spiritual advising consists of giving good news—God loves, forgives, and embraces us as His own children. Christlikeness is highly desirable. Christ's life is appealing. People are drawn to the personality, virtue, and integrity of Jesus. The spiritual adviser recommends Christ Jesus—His way of living joyfully, of being useful, of loving others. As God becomes clear to people, they are drawn like a magnet to Him.

Evangelism is the natural outflow of a vital church. God's people, when they reflect the beauty of Jesus, have a great impact upon the lives of others. The unbeliever feels the warmth of Christian kindness in the body of believers and may in time see the God behind human acts of mercy, service, and encouragement. The church acting as Jesus did attracts people.

Praise and worship are also ways in which the church pictures God for others. One task of the congregation is to describe God in ways that cause seekers to be attracted to Him. Evangelism, to be effective, understands that people make a decision to live for God because of how they feel about God. The psalmist invites us, "Magnify the LORD with me, and let us exalt his name together" (Ps. 34:3, KJV).

Jim

That crisp autumn morning in 1975 was a life-changing one for me. As the sun broke through the morning clouds, I was

The Christian's Response to the Pre-Christian

The conversation of the pre-Christian determines the methods and processes of evangelism. The Christian witness must listen and respond appropriately.

CONVERSATIONS OF THE PRE-CHRISTIAN	RESPONSES OF THE CHRISTIAN WITNESS	PROCESS OF EVANGELISM
	Presence Evangelism	
• Sure, I believe in God.	• I try to live the life.	• Credibility of the Christian is being established.
• I don't know the Bible.		
• I didn't grow up in church.	• I'm praying for my unsaved friends.	
• I've wondered about God and the Bible.		• Contact with the world.
• I know I ought to learn more about God.	• I model Christan living.	
• Can you answer a question for me?	• I do nice things for unsaved people.	• Compassion or acts of kindness are shared.
	Proclamation Evangelism	
• I know God loves me.	• I explain what Jesus means to me.	• Communication of the Good News.
• The Bible says I need to accept Christ.	• I tell about the time Christ came into my life.	
• If I get saved, I know I will need to make some changes.	• I recount how Jesus died for everyone.	• Counseling people about spiritual matters.
	Persuasion Evangelism	
• I know I should get saved.	• I ask if they are ready to accept Christ.	• Challenging people to respond to God's offer of relationship.
• I need to get right with God.		
• I think I'm ready to accept Christ.	• I tell them I hope they will become Christians soon.	
• Will you pray with me?		

Presence Evangelism	Christians continue to build their relationship with the pre-Christian, modeling Christ's love. Christian witnesses show genuine concern for prospective believers and seek ways to meet their needs.
Proclamation Evangelism	Christians share what they have seen, heard, and experienced of God. Often conversations simply turn from surface to spiritual matters. During proclamation the Christian is always listening and praying for an opportunity to share how God has or is working.
Persuasion Evangelism	Christians encourage pre-Christians to accept Christ. Christians also explain how to accept Christ and invite them into relationship with God.

From *Finding Our MAP (Mission Achieving Potential)*. © 1994 Church Growth Research Center, Southern Nazarene University.

"putting out a fleece" by making a special vow to God: on that day I would attempt to lead someone to faith in Jesus Christ. That kind of promise now seems brash and immature. But that morning in my college dorm room, it came at the end of a series of events God was using in shaping my faith.

I had recently received word that two friends of mine from high school days had died in two separate car accidents, both in a relatively short period of time. Suddenly it became so clear to me how life can be so very fragile and temporary.

The bold promise I made that morning had grown partly out of frustration. I was concerned that in all my years as a Christian, I had never intentionally tried to make a formal presentation of the gospel to anyone. After two years of Bible college, completing a motivating course on personal evangelism, and spending a summer as a short-term foreign missionary, I still had never tried to lead anyone to Christ.

The parables of Jesus on "the lost and found" in Luke 15 had spoken dramatically to me. To realize nothing brought more celebration in heaven than bringing a person to faith! I saw how sharing faith is close to God's heart and has eternal consequences. How thrilling to know that through our obedience other people could be in heaven one day!

All those thoughts were stirring in my mind. That afternoon I unexpectedly met a man named Joe while searching for a used auto part. Eventually I found the courage to share with him. I completely forgot the "correct presentation" from our evangelism class. The explanation was out of sequence, and most of the verses were mismatched. I was so nervous I could hardly carry on the conversation.

You cannot imagine my surprise when Joe said he wanted to pray with me and receive Christ into his life! After we prayed together in the middle of that auto yard, he told me his story. He said, "I'm just visiting in the area—I live out of state. My car broke down last night after I got to town. This was the only place I could find parts to fix my car. I'm here because my wife left me last week, and I came here to her parent's house to try to talk with her—but I know what I've really needed is having God in my life."

And it suddenly became so clear that sharing faith is not something we do on our own. The power in faith sharing is that

God is working through our clumsy attempts in ways we cannot begin to predict or understand. As we remain faithful and "connected" with Him, the life-giving truth we express bears fruit in others, as Jesus taught in John 15. And as God the Father shapes and prunes our faith, we can begin to bear more fruit—even much fruit—for His glory.

I hurried back to the campus, excited about the experience. When I met the student dorm resident at the back door of the dorm, I told him the story of Joe coming to faith. He said, "I'm graduating this year and under appointment as a missionary. But I've never personally led anyone to faith in Christ. Will you go with me and present the gospel to someone else?"

I thought my heart would stop. But in our youthful enthusiasm and inexperience, we got our Testaments and headed to town to share a gospel presentation with someone—in fact, anyone who would listen. Before the afternoon was over, the Lord led us to four different people who accepted Christ as their personal Savior. One was a 17-year-old who had secretly packed his car after a distressing argument with his father. He was running away from home and had stopped for a sandwich where we were having lunch. After receiving Christ, he said he knew his problem wasn't his dad—his problem had been in his own life. He then drove home to unpack his car and make things right with his father.

Sharing faith with others shapes our own faith.

That unusual day began to help me understand how vitally important it is to share faith, both for others and for our own spiritual development. Sharing faith with others shapes faith in us.

Since that eventful day, the Holy Spirit has been shaping my understanding about how to approach people in meaningful ways to share faith with them. Some of what we did that day was unique, but some of those truths have continued to guide me to the present in sharing the gospel.

Be motivated by a genuine love for people.

Nothing is more attractive or encouraging to people looking for spiritual answers in their lives than your understanding and acceptance. By treating those we want to reach for Christ with respect and really listening to their concerns, we open up communication lines with them. We can begin a dialogue on developing faith that allows them to deal with their spiritual questions and misunderstandings. Far too many people have resisted coming to faith in Christ because of the poor attitudes and mistreatment they experienced from misguided believers in presenting faith to them.

Forget winning arguments. Focus on winning hearts.

The familiar axiom is true that "People don't care how much you know until they know how much you care." Nothing can ever take the place of genuine compassion and concern for the spiritual needs of others. Forget winning arguments and focus on winning hearts.

The apostle Paul taught us as believers to "warmly welcome each other into the church, just as Christ has warmly welcomed you; then God will be glorified" (Rom. 15:7, TLB). It is the mercy of God that leads the lost to repentance, not His judgment or even our condemnation. Jesus taught that He did not come to condemn the world, but to save it.

Deal with their "stick points."

Sharing faith can be a long process of partnering with God to impact others in life changes. Many times the reason a person has never put his or her trust in Christ is that he or she is struggling with multiple issues or even a misunderstanding about God. One of the ways to effectively approach people in sharing your faith is to watch and listen for their spiritual "stick points." Then be ready to help walk them through those areas of concern.

As you become aware of those areas, you can help process their questions over time. In fact, by allowing them time to think and pray through these faith challenges, they are more likely to stick to their faith.

Sharing faith is helping people take those first steps toward faith and dealing with the challenges they are facing in trusting God.

Operate from your spiritual giftedness.

One of the ways to approach others in sharing faith is according to your own spiritual enabling. Many times we act as if the gifts of the Spirit center only on the care and nurture of believers. And while it's true that many of the gifts are designed for the good of a local body of believers, they should not need to be used exclusively inside the fellowship of the church. Spiritual gifts can be an excellent bridge for faith.

Perhaps one way to determine how you could approach an unbelieving friend or acquaintance is through doing what you do best. Express Christ's love to that person by helping him or her in some thoughtful way. One new believer decided he could chop firewood for his unchurched friends. Another made it a point to shovel the sidewalks of his older neighbors after a heavy snow. Love them until they ask you, "Why?" and then be ready to explain in a clear and meaningful way that your faith is the reason for your outlook on life.

Who you are impacts how you serve. Live out who God made you to be. Share faith from your areas of strength and spiritual gifts.

Watch for God's clues.

Since we are partnering with God in this challenge of faith shaping and sharing, we can depend upon His help and guidance. As we do our best to be prepared to share our faith in meaningful ways, we must also remember that He gives life.

As the scripture teaches, one plants and another waters, but it's God who brings the increase. The miracle of life does not come from our skills or abilities, but from God. The moving of His Spirit is often a mystery. Jesus compared it to the blowing winds that we are unable to see or predict. We can only observe the results.

So as we are in tune to the moving of God, we are guided to know when to approach some people. Timing is vital in effectively sharing faith. One day we will fully understand God's delays and His timing, but He has given us many earthly examples of how the timing must be right.

One of the stories recycled regularly in our family reunions was about a well-meaning uncle. Seems that when he was a boy, he discovered a well-hidden nest of prized turkey eggs. To his delight, they were beginning to hatch, so he thought he would help them along. He broke open the shells for the baby turkeys, since they seemed to be having such a rough time and taking so long. Of course, he really did them no favor. The struggle to escape their egg shells actually strengthens hatchlings to face their new world. Few of the young brood survived his well-intentioned but misguided intervention.

The struggles to come to faith seem to have a similar mystery of life. God in His time with our obedience and response brings the miracle of new life. We need only be in tune with His time. The struggle is all part of the process to new life. At times we may be tempted to help out by improperly intervening in this process of faith. But as we are in tune with the work of God's Spirit and partner with His plans, the miracle of new life can happen.

10

"What Am I to Say When 'There Are Lots of Ways to God'?"

> *The requirement for us . . . is that the Christian gospel should be voiced and heard as:*
> - *intellectually credible in an unreflective society;*
> - *politically critical and constructive in a cynical community;*
> - *pastorally attentive in a society of easy but fake answers.*
> —Walter Brueggemann
> *Biblical Perspectives on Evangelism*

Lyle

It's fashionable these days to end religious conversations by saying, "I guess there are lots of ways to God." Such conversations often conclude at this point, because many Christians are puzzled as to what to say next.

Suppose we were to say, "No, there's only one way to God, and that's through Jesus Christ." You would expect one or more of a few devastating reactions, such as the end of the conversation, a disgusting shaking of the head, an accusation of elitism or intolerance.

It's a lot easier for us to say nothing or to settle with the time-honored cliché "Let's agree to disagree." With such an agreement our emotions are comforted; the potential conflict is averted.

Personally we are only mildly satisfied, however, with such an easy and simple conclusion. If we reflect, we begin to ask ourselves, "Why do I believe anything at all if it doesn't matter what

I believe?" Answers don't come quickly to such an in-depth question, so most of the time we quit trying to find answers. We pacify ourselves by saying, "At least we were able to keep from arguing with other people. After all, friendship is vitally important." Many of us have settled for a "live and let live" philosophy of life. We're comfortable saying, "You have your beliefs; I have mine."

The prevailing thought patterns in American society fall under two categories today. These socially accepted ways of thinking thwart witnessing attempts by Christians.

Many people no longer see the Bible as authoritative.

Relativism is the first thought pattern, the implication that there is no objective truth. That is, everyone can believe as he or she wants to believe. One's own personal opinion is the primary authority. For example, many people no longer see the Bible as authoritative on how to live. If they do see the Bible as authoritative, they pick and choose which parts of the Bible they allow to direct their lives. Under the protective shield of relativism, people can excuse and disguise unethical behavior. They defend ungodly behavior by saying, "Well, that's your opinion, and this is mine. That might be true for you, but it's not true for me."

When it comes to biblical Christianity, Christians consider the Bible as God's revelation. We say, "This is objective truth." By that we mean truth comes from outside of us and is God-given. But our society says that truth is not truth until it's subjective, until I see it and sense it from within. So our world is simply saying, "That may be true for you, but it's not true for me."

When Christians hear this response they are often stopped in their tracks. Because what we have considered authoritative—the Bible—is not considered authoritative by another person. Since we don't have a common ground to accept something as true, we don't know the next step.

Common expressions of relativism include "Well, it all depends upon the individual, or the circumstance." "Whatever is right for you is right for you."

Pluralism is the second way of thinking that confuses Christians, the belief that truth can be seen in a variety of ways. This philosophy has two forms. The first is *dogmatic* pluralism, an acceptance of diversity as absolute truth. To suggest that someone needs to change is considered disrespectful to the other person's uniqueness. That way of thinking resists the Christian's attempt to lead someone to Christ. When a Christian starts to witness, some people will say, "Hey—knock it off! We don't need that. Let people be as they are." The overriding philosophy is "live and let live—don't force your religion down my throat."

The second kind of pluralism is *descriptive* pluralism, a recognition and valuing of uniqueness. This line of thinking says, "Not all people are the same, and we appreciate their diversity. We should admire and rejoice in the uniqueness of individuals."

We must not be sidetracked by the proposal, "There are lots of ways to God."

Does God work differently in people's lives? Yes. We must not be sidetracked, however, by the popular saying "There are lots of ways to God." Pluralism is dangerous. There *are* lots of ways to God, depending on what those "ways" include. A thoughtful Christian should ask a couple of questions when he or she hears comments like this. "What do you mean by 'There are lots of ways to God'?" we might ask. "What are some of those ways?"

Most answers will fit three categories. People are likely to say, "You don't have to go to church to be a Christian." In other words, it's possible to be saved outside of the church—to that we would all agree. There were no buildings designated as churches in the New Testament. The church as an organization or as a worship event is not essential to the salvation of souls. Even if the person were to define the church as the people of God, it is possible for the unsaved to accept Christ without the influence of the godly. The Holy Spirit may influence unbelievers apart from Christians—but that's not generally the way He works. Most often He ministers through His people, the Church.

The second thing people might say is, "Look—Judaism, Hinduism, Buddhism, and Islam are acceptable, although probably not the best options. Christianity is the best option, but let's not put down other religions. People in these other religions be-

lieve in God too." The statement "All religions lead to God" as-
sumes the existence of one personal God. But Hindus and Bud-
dhists teach that all things are actually one thing—part of an am-
biguous universal divine principle. And Mormons teach that
people can become gods. We can see that the seemingly simple
thought "There are lots of ways to God" can become complex in
a hurry.

Some people in our society are simply talking about denominations when they make a statement like this. Being a Baptist,
Methodist, Presbyterian, or an adherent of the Church of God or
Assembly of God are, in their minds, *ways* to God. Certainly God
uses a variety of denominations and methods to bring people to
himself. So in one sense we believe in some measure of pluralism.

Christians are eager to acknowledge the creative and mysterious ways of God.

Christians are eager to acknowledge the
creative and even mysterious ways of God
in dealing with people. Some people have
been knocked to their knees by failure or
tragedy. God used the difficulty to bring
these people into a saving relationship. Others flush with the triumph of an achieve-
ment and deep personal fulfillment saw that
God had enabled them to reach the pinnacle
of success. With humility of heart, they
vowed before the Lord to seek His face. God
has used friends and enemies, criticism and compliments, com-
munities of faith and resistant cliques to draw people into the
Kingdom.

A third possible meaning to "There are lots of ways to God"
is "I believe the good in my life outweighs the bad." The Christian would say, "Absolutely not" to trusting good works to bring
a person into God's favor. This philosophy allows people to feel
in control—they determine what makes them acceptable to God.
This self-trust is contrary to the Good News.

When the Christian witness is confronted with "There are
lots of ways to God," he or she would do well to find out what
the person really means. Frequently the person who says this is
simply parroting what he or she has heard others say.

A positive way to respond when people say this is "You

know, I think I agree with you, but tell me what you mean by that," because we probably do agree with them. But let's make sure.

Suppose, however, the person says, "I believe if you do good things . . ." We can respond, "That's interesting, but may I explain why I'm a little uncomfortable with what you're saying?" Then we can talk about how the Bible says a person is not saved by good works. "I've discovered it's better than that," we can reply. "God tells us we can be close to Him by faith instead of by effort." By gently speaking, we can counter relativism and dogmatic pluralism by simply explaining Jesus' good news.

Let's give a little thought to two concerns: (1) We must polish and refine our belief system, based upon something other than simply tradition, church, family, and comfort. Sometimes we form beliefs on a practical evaluation, such as "They work for me." We rarely consider that our beliefs need to be refined and polished by both the Church and the world.

A man of another religion began to ask questions about my belief in the afterlife. He was attempting to set me up by making me commit to a particular theory of heaven and hell. Sensing that I was aware of what he was attempting to do, he said, "I don't mean to put you in a corner about your beliefs."

I responded to him, "If my beliefs don't bear up under scrutiny or if my thoughts are in some way inconsistent with the Bible, then I need to find firm footing." In other words, I gave him permission to challenge my beliefs, to correct my thinking, to disagree with me. With my declared interest in learning, our conversation continued with both of us relaxed (although I declined to become very definitive about my theory of the end of time, for so much of it is speculative).

Jesus entrusted great truths to those uneducated, as well as to the informed.

(2) Our beliefs are not fully ours until we're able to express them in ways people understand. We may have random thoughts or even a reasonable collection of ideas that make sense to us. Until we're able to explain them clearly, we're probably not deeply convinced of their value for others. Some of us, however, feel we must be able to explain things deeply or profoundly. This is not nec-

essary. Much of our theology is a simple explanation of God's relationship with us.

While we may hold a deep appreciation for people who study theology in-depth and are able to explain it with profundity, we are reminded that Jesus entrusted great truths to uneducated fishermen, as well as to the brilliant and educated apostle Paul.

"It doesn't matter what you believe as long as you're sincere." This statement is another expression of pluralism that makes witnessing seem futile. The futility comes because it seems that people *sincerely* believe whatever it is they believe—if it is obviously wrong, they probably wouldn't believe it!

The position that sincerity, rather than truth, is to be embraced may be taken because it seems too difficult to think through why we believe as we do. Or it could be that we're overwhelmed by the diversity of options as to what to believe, so we settle for the freedom of individual choice with accompanying personal dedication to that belief. Or, more than likely, we permit a large variety of belief options, because tolerance is seen to be more acceptable than presumptive confidence. The real issue may be that we have no outside source of authority upon which both believers and unbelievers can agree. Therefore, any sincerely held opinion must be acceptable. After all, "Who is to say what's right or wrong?"

The rise of pluralism is due among other things to a lack of trusted authority or source of truth. At one time in our history, the Church was considered authoritative. Matters of life and relationship could be brought to the clergy, who would then address questions of morality and priority. With the decreasing influence of the Church has come an increasing number of value systems. Today it is very difficult to agree on how one should behave.

With the decline of the authority of the Church came the rise of the authority of the Bible. But the Bible has been questioned as to its ability to relate to the contemporary scene. And now people question which parts of the Bible should be embraced and which should be rejected. These days I'm hearing statements such as "Oh, I believe the Bible. But I pick and choose which ideas I live by."

With the overthrow of any established authority comes the natural result—"Everyone did what was right in his own eyes" (Judg. 21:25, NKJV). So our society, like Israel of old, has rejected all principles except the one: "All values are relative."

With the embracing of such a philosophy of life—namely that there are no governing principles of right or wrong (except that which is legal or illegal), the social climate has changed. We are now afraid of offering our beliefs about Christ lest we embarrass, hurt, or drive people away. We have developed a social sensitivity that serves as a restraint to religious conversation. A church leader, expressing this development in the American culture, said, "Talking to people about religion in America is as offensive as eating stew with your fingers." Although people would prefer being silent to being laughed at, scorned, or put down, the greater issue seems to be a sensitivity about the feelings of others who may not agree.

What then are we to do? We are to become advocates of a relationship with Christ that is informed by the Bible. Relativism and pluralism actually open the door to our opinions, positions, and beliefs. We are to air our views kindly and frequently. We're to speak of God and let Him drive home the truth about himself. We need not argue people into accepting our position. Rather, we are to become proclaimers of what we believe. Knowing that God convinces people of right living and of truth, we allow our words to be used by Him to touch the lives of others.

We are to air our views kindly and frequently.

We have a strong basis for proclaiming a right relationship through Jesus Christ. We have a historical Christ who lived and died and was resurrected to live eternally. Much evidence supports this claim. Furthermore, Christianity makes sense of human nature. Christianity works, that is, it provides helpful guidelines for daily living in ways that are compatible with our human makeup and societal dynamics. In other words, we have some objective evidence with which to work as we talk to people about God. We do not have to slip into the muddy waters of relativism to attempt to explain how Christ wants to be a part of our lives.

On the other hand, we must never imagine that people are going to suddenly become Christians because we've mentioned God's workings in our lives. We must be reminded of the agricultural model and the various roles necessary in harvesting a crop. Someone must cultivate the soil, another plant the seed, another nurture the young plant, another supply water and nutrients to the soil. Then and only then can the harvest take place.

We're to propose a loving relationship with Christ. Our times call us to recommend aggressively a relationship with Christ. We're to propose a loving relationship with Christ. Our advocacy must be without elitism. We must humbly listen to other positions and beliefs. We're to accept people of other faiths without arguing or agreeing. But we're to make topics of religion open to conversation, exploration, and analysis. While people are shifting from one position to another, we're to be supportive of them in their decision-making process. All the while we're to explain who Jesus is and how He is relevant for our day in terms of hope, security, and love.

We Christians can find a way through the land mines of the socially inept who offensively babble about God. We are to shrug off the self-imposed silence that alerts no one to our allegiance to Christ. Could the pathway to successful Christian witnessing include this invitation—"Taste and see that the LORD is good" (Ps. 34:8)?

11

"How Do I Become a Spiritual Adviser?"

As iron sharpens iron, so one man sharpens another.
—Prov. 27:17

Jim

Not long after moving to southern California, we discovered that driving a car was different here than in any other place we had ever known. Fortunately we did not have to make long commutes to work every day, but occasionally we had to venture out onto the interstates to make an early morning meeting. Have you ever seen a 10-lane parking lot at rush hours?

We became highly motivated to use what they call the "diamond lanes" on the main interstate freeways and the "fast track" on the toll roads. These lanes to the far left are reserved for vehicles carrying two or more persons. Additionally, the toll roads allow for discounts for those with multiple passengers.

Speaking from experience, I must say that there's only one thing more discouraging than sitting bumper to bumper in rush-hour traffic when as far as you can see ahead nothing's moving. That's glancing over to the left lane and watching the "fast trackers" whiz by all the stalled traffic. Those commuters are usually laughing and talking together, sipping on a travel mug of hot coffee—almost as if they knew we were watching them, helplessly stuck in our misery.

For those unfamiliar with this highway system, the first response is to jump into the diamond lane out of sheer frustration. Recently a friend of mine was in traffic court and overheard that the judge was handing out fines to those pulled over for diamond lane violations. Some were $1,000, and some were even more. That's why hundreds of drivers stay in the long lines, obeying the highway laws. The price of breaking them is much too great.

I've often wondered why anyone who had to commute to work every day would want to sit in all that bumper-to-bumper traffic for hours. Why not find someone else in their office to car-pool with so they could use the diamond lanes? Why would anyone be content to edge along a few inches at a time every day while those beside them were flying by unaffected by their dilemma?

Sure, those with out-of-state license plates have a good excuse. They had no idea what they were getting into when they ventured onto that freeway on-ramp at 8 A.M. But thousands of residents choose to go through the same frustrating experience day after day, week after week, and month after month. That probably explains "the road rage" in our part of the country and why people move every two or three years. It seems to be human nature just to do nothing and adapt to the inconveniences. I've seen it every day on the California highway systems. And I'm continuing to see it every week in the spiritual formation of believers.

You see, there is also a "fast track" for spiritual formation and development. God has provided a way for believers to accelerate their spiritual growth and find the gems and jewels for life in the heavenly diamond lane of Christian experience. The New Testament describes this spiritual car pool in the "one another passages." Repeatedly we are encouraged by the Scriptures to "encourage one another," "pray for one another," "love one another," "forgive one another," "build up one another," "stir up one another to good works," "bear with one another," and "carry one another's burdens."

We were created for fellowship with God and with one another.

God never intended that we make our spiritual journey alone, frustrated and isolated. Faith is best shaped and formed in the context of a biblical community. We were created for fellowship with God and one another. The only time in the creation story that God looked at His creation with dissatisfaction was when He observed that man was alone. The sense of being together is at the very core of our nature. Our journey will be easier and more enjoyable in the company of other believers!

So why is it that any Christians today feel alone in their spiritual journey? The greatest reason may be as simple as understanding your reaction to the title of this chapter. Most believers do not consider themselves capable of being a spiritual adviser to anyone. They would be quick to say, "I can't be a spiritual coach or adviser. I'm not ready for that yet. I have too many weaknesses and problems to be able to help someone else."

These same people would be very interested in having someone else advise them. Nearly every Christian would say, "I could really benefit from having a mentor or spiritual adviser in my life—someone I could talk to about the issues in my faith and how to accelerate my spiritual progress." Most of us would see ourselves on the receiving end of this kind of relationship but hesitate to consider being on the giving end. Somehow it seems proud or too assuming.

Faith is best formed through relationships. But let's reconsider that perspective for a moment and review what we know about the formation of faith. We know that throughout the Bible God developed faith in the life of His people by using spiritual advisers. In the Old Testament Moses trained Joshua, Elijah mentored Elisha, and Eli guided the prophet in training young Samuel. In the New Testament Jesus selected the disciples and apostles; Paul trained Barnabas, Silas, Timothy, and many others. The pattern is repeated many times over. Faith is best formed through meaningful relationships with other believers.

Bob Biehl writes in his classic *Mentoring: Confidence in Finding a Mentor and Becoming One*, "Mentors look inside us and find the person we long to be. Then they help to bring that to life. At their best, they nurture our souls. They shape our character. They call us to be complete and whole, and by the grace of God, holy. Have you been sharpened against the whetstone of another's wisdom and character?"

The instruction of the apostle Paul to his own spiritual partner in ministry, the younger Timothy, is timeless in its truth and impact.

You must teach others those things you and many others have heard me speak about. Teach these great truths to trustworthy men who will, in turn, pass them on to others (2 Tim. 2:2, TLB).

What we sometimes miss in this verse is the picture of the spiritual relay that is going on. As others have impacted our lives and encouraged our spiritual formation, we are to do the same.

I watched my oldest daughter's high school track team recently at a winning meet. The relay teams were well-trained and talented and won every event. Soon it became a matter of pride to see how far ahead the anchor could finish the race. The coaches seemed to save the best and fastest runners for that last leg of the relay. But it took each runner carrying the baton to the next teammate for the race to be won. If just one runner stopped, it didn't matter how fast and capable the others were—the race would be over.

The sharing of faith has the same dynamic at work. Each generation of believers and spiritual leaders must faithfully deliver the faith to the next generation of leaders who are waiting. We all become both teachers and students in this process. Our abilities or skills may not be as good as that of some of our students. We may sense a feeling of intimidation about our progress compared to their talents. But if the race is to be won, we must pass on the faith to others. As God brought others to advise and guide us spiritually, we need to live out our gratitude by doing the same.

In faith ventures, we receive more than we invest.

As is usually the case, when we venture into this kind of faith partnership, we receive more than we give to it. Ventures of faith have a predictable way of giving back more than we invest. Newly activated spiritual advisers are surprised to discover what an enriching experience this ministry becomes to their own faith. The Kingdom principle seems to be that God will always multiply and return what we invest in love and devotion for Him. It is true in the stewardship of life. It is proven in the ministry of our spiritual gifts or the investment of our time and energy for His work. And it is particularly true in the mentoring relationships we cultivate and develop.

One of the challenges we share in The Family Church is utilizing this principle as we train our teachers. One of the most effective ways to learn is through teaching. Many of our members are new Christians and feel insecure about helping in our Sunday School classes. "I don't know the Bible well enough," they say. "I need to learn more and grow spiritually before I can be a teacher or a class assistant in training." We've discovered that an excellent way for new believers to learn the Bible is to help teach a class of children. As they assist in the class, study parts of the lessons to teach and eventually teach a whole lesson, they learn more quickly than they ever would have just by listening or reading the Bible alone.

It's the idea of "Give, and it will be given to you" (Luke 6:38). In fact, perhaps the greatest choice you could make in your own spiritual formation would be to choose to become a spiritual coach and adviser to another new Christian. Let's examine some practical steps to help you in this process.

Pray about your faith partner.

Ask the Lord to show you the right person for this ministry. No doubt there are many around you who would benefit from your friendship and spiritual partnership. By praying about this decision, the Lord can begin to sensitize you to those you may not have been aware of in your world of relationships and webs of influence.

Ask someone if he or she is interested.

How would you feel if someone you respected approached you one day and said, "I've been praying about partnering with someone who will join me in growing personal faith. I feel impressed to ask you to consider meeting with me over the next several months at a convenient time so we can discuss ways to grow spiritually"?

Give the person some time to consider your invitation. Make sure he or she is motivated to enter into this partnership and that it's not just your idea. If the person is truly interested, his or her involvement will be more enthusiastic as you plan to meet together.

Review some guidelines together.

In their book titled *Connecting: The Mentoring Relationships You Need to Succeed in Life,* authors Stanley and Clinton outline what they call the "Ten Commandments of Mentoring." They are adapted for our use here and provide some helpful guidelines for building a partnership in faith shaping. By building your awareness in these areas, your efforts can be more productive in a mentoring relationship.

1. *Value the relationship.* The stronger the mentoring relationship, the greater the empowerment. Compatibility and chemistry are true advantages, especially in co-mentoring with a ministry peer. Most relationships will not grow to a close friendship, and they don't need to. But it's important to continue to develop the relationship.

2. *Talk about your expectations.* When mentoring efforts prove disappointing, the problems are frequently traced back to differing or unfulfilled expectations. Commandments 3-8 deal with important areas of expectations.

3. *Establish a regular meeting schedule.* A meeting every six to eight weeks could begin your efforts and be adjusted as you both desire. Also, set your ground rules for your meeting routines and availability for impromptu contacts.

4. *Determine your accountability style.* Mutual accountability is something each mentoring team should establish. Agree together on how you will set and monitor the topics and tasks you wish to discuss.

5. *Set up your communication tools.* How and when to communicate areas of challenge or correction should be clarified early in a mentoring relationship. With peers, a covenant can assist with this value.

6. *Clarify the level of confidentiality.* If this faith partnership deepens, it may involve sharing personal matters between the two partners. One or both may not want these things conveyed to others outside this relationship. Both need to make it clear as to when something you share should be treated as confidential.

7. *Set time limits.* Some basic guidelines should be understood not only for the length of this mentoring relationship—say, up to 24 months—but also for the length of your regular meetings. Recognize the necessity of time limitations.

8. *Evaluate your progress regularly.* Evaluation is primarily a function in spiritual formation. Consider the components of attraction, responsiveness, and accountability. A joint evaluation can assist both people in measuring progress and growth.

9. *Set realistic expectations.* Expectations are primarily the responsibility of the student. Evaluation and feedback can modify any unrealistic expectations and assist in making this relationship a fulfilling experience.

10. *Bring closure to the mentoring relationship.* This is probably the most violated of all the commandments. Build a clear understanding at the start of the relationship about the eventual closure. Being able to know the guidelines in entering such a partnership will enable more people to respond positively to the invitation.

God has a delightful way of bringing the right people across our paths at just the right time. Some are able to put us on a fast track of spiritual development that saves us so much wasted time when we're learning primarily from our own experience. It is wise to learn from experience, but it's even wiser to learn from the experience of others.

God also directs across our paths others who are looking for the answers to the questions we have already worked through in our lives. Through the natural give and take in such friendships, our spirits are enriched and faith is shaped in significant ways as we assist them through the same process.

The baton of faith is passed from one generation to the next.

12

"Who's Going to Help Me with My Family?"

> Those who sow in tears will reap with songs of joy. He who goes out weeping, carrying seed to sow, will return with songs of joy, carrying sheaves with him.
>
> —Ps. 126:5-6

Jim

A case study of a large and growing community came to my attention recently as it catalogued a number of disturbing trends in family life. As the needs in this case study are described, you may be able to identify some families you know who are going through the same kinds of pressures and stress points. This interesting study focused particularly on several families who have become highly visible and in the public consciousness.

Before we give you their names, please remember their family situations are unique for three reasons: (1) They lived in the same community. (2) Several of the families would be acknowledged to be among the rich and famous. (3) A common characteristic was discovered in all these families, one that had initially prompted the case study.

The case study listed the families' names, made general references about where the families lived and worked, and then described their problems. The report made me somewhat uncomfortable for all of them, wondering if they would ever come to regret this level of transparency and vulnerability. The study's listing of family dysfunctions included the following:

- Two stepchildren were caught in the turmoil of blended family conflict.

- Not far away, the grown siblings of another household were completely estranged because they disagreed over dividing the family's inheritance.
- An older couple grieved over their only son. He was highly gifted and a near genius intellectually but was wasting his life away with no moral boundaries and seemingly no goals or ambitions.
- Another family was trying to cope with the murder of one of their children.
- An economically disadvantaged family struggled to survive, as the mother had left the world of prostitution and was trying desperately to start a new life.
- One of the families was split in unresolved conflict over differing religious views and practices.

In some ways, it sounds like Anytown, U.S.A., doesn't it? It almost reads like the story line for some novel or television drama. Let's continue:

- A federal judge climbed the social ladder to overcome many economic and cultural ills found in his community.
- A leader in the national political scene had an uncontrollable son who brought shame to the family's name and legacy.
- A couple was locked in highly visible legal battles over malpractice issues involving their treatments for infertility problems.

What amazed me at first was that these families would allow their private problems to become so public, almost common knowledge. The second aspect of this study that made me do a double take was the one thing they all held in common.

Have you recognized any of these families yet based on the above descriptions?

Let me share with you what they had in common before revealing their identities. The common denominator for all these hurting homes is their deeply religious and spiritual values. Their strong faith in God dramatically contrasted with their disturbing family issues.

In many ways you could say they were models for other families to study and follow. The author's purpose for the case study was to provide real-life examples of people whose pain had helped shape faith in the lives and particularly in their own families.

This case study was written about 2,000 years ago. The community was the biblical community of faith. The research analyst for the study was the apostle Paul, and we've named the case study "the faith chapter," found in Heb. 11. Here are the family identities. All are mentioned in Heb. 11 and are considered to be heroes of our faith:

- The two stepchildren with blended family conflict: Isaac and Ishmael.
- The family with the murdered child: Adam and Eve.
- The estranged adult children with inheritance issues: Jacob and Esau.
- The highly gifted and near genius son with boundary issues in morality: Samson.
- Cain killed Abel over his differing religious views and practices.
- Rahab had been a prostitute to provide for her family before following Jehovah.
- Gideon was the federal judge from the poorest family in the lowest tribe in Israel.
- The national political leader shamed by his son's rebellion: King David.
- The couple with infertility problems and legal battles that are still going on today were Abraham and Sarah.

Obviously, the problems these people faced are not unique. We all know families in these same kinds of problems many years later. But what *is* encouraging to us is that God looks at these people in the midst of their distressing family dysfunctions and says, "These believers are real faith heroes!"

God's viewpoint becomes a great source of comfort to believers for many reasons. One of the greatest is that for most of us it seems the people we are closest to can seem the most difficult to impact in faith.

As believers we want to ask God to *fix* our loved ones, or *change* them, or *heal* them, or *transform* them. But Heb. 11 teaches us what we should want God to do for our family. In the context of these family situations and stresses, read these verses, thinking of the various life situations that have been described: *Now faith means that we have full confidence in the things we hope for, it means being certain of things we cannot see* (Heb. 11:1, PHILLIPS)

Doubt decides what God can't do; faith frees us to see what God will do.

Even in the kinds of family situations these heroes of our faith endured, we can have a "full confidence." The temptation for Christians is to decide what God *can't* do by looking at life through our fears. But we decide what God *can* do by looking at our family's needs and hurts through eyes of faith. Doubt decides what God can't do; faith frees us to embrace what God *can* do.

If these heroes listed in Faith's Hall of Fame could share and shape faith in their family situations, then maybe we can too.

At times we may feel that the people we love the most in our immediate or extended circle of family and friends are the most difficult to shape in their faith. Yet the truth is, we have a great deal of influence over the people we love the most. We make a difference in their lives, and we can help bring them to faith in Jesus and then encourage them in their spiritual growth.

The temptation is to try to make shaping and sharing faith for our families a "one size fits all." Most believers pray and carry a burden for reaching their loved ones and family for Christ. These families of faith teach us some timeless truths.

Faith knows God can open up a way.

Abraham was a great illustration of this principle:

It was by faith that Abraham obeyed the call to set out for a country that was the inheritance given to him and his descendants, and that he set out without knowing where he was going (Heb. 11:8, JB).

Faith goes deeper than just mentally accepting something as true. Genuine faith moves us into action, at times before we have all the answers. Abraham trusted what he knew was right and believed God would show him a way to go. His faith was based on the conviction that he would know enough from the Lord when the time was right.

As we read through this case study of faith in Heb. 11, it becomes evident that tests and trials were used by God to reflect authentic faith for the world to see. We sometimes misunderstand the stress points of life—that somehow they disqualify us in being people of "real faith." But the faith chapter shows us that God uses what appears to be obstacles as opportunities for faith to become more evident. We can move ahead in sharing faith with our family without knowing exactly where or how it will all come together.

The Red Sea was the vehicle for the deliverance for God's people and the destruction of their enemies. Have you ever realized that God could use obstacles to faith in your family the same way?

"Who can help me with reaching my family?" God can, and God will.

One of the thrills of the journey of faith is watching God use the various problems in our families as a way to share and shape faith.

Faith knows God never gives up on us.

Have you discovered yet that life has a way of draining your dreams and freezing your faith? What happens when your prayers are not being answered? How do you handle it when the family member you want to reach seems unresponsive and unaffected by all your efforts to share faith in a meaningful way?

People who are effective in sharing faith must learn to feed their own faith. They discover what they need to keep that sense of expectation alive. While the formula may be varied for each believer, each of us can discover what sparks new hope in our times of delays in answers to prayer.

Some claim a promise or truth from God's Word. They have learned the valuable lesson that faith can feed and grow on eternal truths.

God *is able to . . . do superabundantly, far over and above all that we [dare] ask or think [infinitely beyond our highest prayers, desires, thoughts, hopes, or dreams]*— (Eph. 3:20, AMP.).

These things I plan won't happen right away. Slowly, steadily, surely, the time approaches when the vision will be fulfilled. If it seems slow, do not despair, for these things will surely come to pass. Just be patient! They will not be overdue a single day! (Hab. 2:3, TLB).

Let us not become weary in doing good, for at the proper time we will reap a harvest if we do not give up (Gal. 6:9).

What is it that reminds you of God's enduring grace and

love? He never gives up on a situation or on a family member. God's grace is available for each family's spiritual need. Nothing is too difficult. His grace is able. His Spirit is faithful. No one is beyond His reach.

Families are changed as members become new creations in Christ Jesus. The gospel of transformation works from the inside out. We do not always see what God is doing in changing people, but faith does not need to see to believe. Faith believes before it sees.

We like to use a stopwatch while God may use a calendar.

How we wrestle with the time issues when it comes to faith issues! We live in a world that demands express lanes at the grocery store, microwaves in the kitchen, live coverage on news programs, and instant E-mail at the office. The whole concept of "waiting before God" sounds illogical today. In matters of faith, we prefer a stopwatch while God may use a calendar.

When it comes to shaping faith and effectively sharing it, God's timing is perfect. He never quits or gives up, and neither can we. Faith breathes that truth.

Faith knows God is always right.

Faith is fully convinced—to the point of conviction—that God is in control. His plan is perfect, and we can count on His rightness, or more correctly, His righteousness.

Consider Isa. 55:8-9:

This plan of mine is not what you would work out, neither are my thoughts the same as yours! For just as the heavens are higher than the earth, so are my ways higher than yours, and my thoughts than yours (TLB).

This scriptural principle makes it clear that we don't always understand how God is working behind the scenes. The final designs He is weaving may not be as beautiful and clear to us on the backside of eternity's tapestry. But after all the confusing circumstances and family problems have left us wondering what He is doing, we ultimately come back to the truth that, as Fanny J. Crosby wrote, "I know, whate'er befall me, / Jesus doeth all things well."

When we followed God's lead to move from the Midwest to southern California in order to start a new church, we asked God for one thing: to protect our family from "the spiritual fallout" of starting a new church. Our new congregation has been wonderful to lead and most considerate and protective of our family in these past six years.

But in the early days it did not go quite so smoothly. We hadn't been in California long before we realized our girls weren't accepting the move as positively as we had hoped. Rachel was nine years old and Lydia was five at the time. They had to share a bed at night in our new little three-room apartment. Each night when Rhonda and I would tuck them in, Rachel would make her bed on the floor. When we asked for an explanation, she would say, "I don't like it here in California. I miss my old house and my own room. I want to see my friends and all the people I miss."

This went on night after night for several weeks. We talked with her and prayed with her. We waited and explained. And then we waited some more. Finally, I sent out a letter to our prayer partners across the nation and included this shrouded request, "Please pray for our family's adjustment here in southern California."

We prepared the mailing to nearly a thousand partners and sent it out early in the week. Later toward the end of the week, I went in one evening to tell the girls good night. I'll never forget what I saw when I stepped in the doorway—the floor. No blankets and pillows in a makeshift bed, but two daughters giggling in bed together and grinning from ear to ear.

"Not sleeping on the floor tonight, Honey?" I asked, unsure what to make of the unannounced change.

"No, Daddy. I think I'm sleeping with Lydia from now on." I did the usual tucks and pats, trying to disguise my delight, and sat down on the edge of the bed.

Without any prompting she went on: "You know, Daddy, I really do like California. It's so nice and warm. Today we saw our new school, and I made a new friend in our apartments. She's coming over to play tomorrow."

While they both chattered on, I wondered who it was who faithfully prayed for our family that week. Somewhere prayer partners had helped shoulder the load and ministered to us, as we had tried to minister to others. Their partnership in faith had made all the difference for our family.

Who is going to help me with my family? God's family can—and will—if we ask them.

Besides trusting God to help us in shaping the faith of our needy or unbelieving family members, we should make it a priority to partner with other believers who can help us shape faith in our families. The gifted Sunday School teacher for your children, a youth worker for your teenager, a men's ministry director for a needy husband, or a ladies' group leader for a wife.

God's family in a local church can be your best partners for shaping faith and sharing faith in your own family. They are not meant to substitute for your influence or your faithful lifestyle, but to accent and reinforce your efforts and prayers. As we minister each week to one another in our local churches, God has a wonderful way of bringing that ministry back to bless and strengthen our own family.

Maybe, just maybe, God will start working through your faith.

13

Shouldn't the Church Be Doing Something Different?

Be wise in the way you act toward outsiders; make the most of every opportunity. Let your conversation be always full of grace, seasoned with salt, so that you may know how to answer everyone.

—Col. 4:5-6

Jim

The familiar buzz of conversation filled the room as our new church prepared for another Sunday morning. The service was about to begin when a first-time guest walked in alone. As I welcomed him, he replied with this statement: "I really don't want to be here today. I'm here only because my counselor insisted I attend. I really don't think I need to go to church. And if I don't like what I'm hearing, I'm going to get up and leave."

At first, Randy's* intense resistance was surprising. We found out later that he had his reasons. Our immediate response was "It's all right if you feel you need to leave—we don't lock the doors after the service begins." That seemed to satisfy his concerns, and he found the closest available seat to the back door.

While this experience may be an extreme example of the defensiveness of new attendees at a weekly worship service, it does

---

*"Randy" and "Rhonda" are fictitious names given to a couple who were part of the The Family Church's target group of unchurched persons in Rancho Santa Margarita, California.

illustrate the reservations many guests have, especially those who attend church rarely, coming into an unfamiliar church.

Anonymity is a valued priority for these weekend spiritual explorers.

These first-timers sit closest to the door. They usually don't want to say anything, sign anything, or join anything in those first several visits. Anonymity is a valued priority for these weekend spiritual explorers.

Interestingly, these uncommitted attendees usually have very low expectations for preaching or worship. While some common concerns exist, they are of a social nature. One door-to-door survey discovered the top four reasons why the people did not attend worship services regularly in our southern California suburbs:

1. The sermons are boring and don't relate to everyday life.
2. The church members are unfriendly to visitors.
3. The churches offer very little for children and youth.
4. All the churches are interested in is money.

In attempting to start and grow a new church, these concerns caught our attention. These four major obstacles to reach and redeem the unchurched had more to do with the approach, style, and ministry context rather than any spiritual issues. We are coming to understand the way we "do church" needs to be winsome and attractive to impact these persons.

Many times we believers misunderstand the reasons why people don't go to church. We tend to think it is because they don't believe in God or accept that the Bible is true. In fact, it has little to do with spiritual issues. Instead, most people who don't have a relationship with the Lord or a church said they felt like outsiders in the churches they had visited.

The more we study the unchurched in our ministry context, the more we realize the challenge we face is translating the truth of the gospel message into "their language." Among some of the more common characteristics of the unchurched are the following:

- They want a church service to be concise and move along at a good pace.
- They want the music styles and songs to match their musical preferences.

- They highly value their sense of individuality.
- They are drawn to church many times for the sake of their children.
- They attend a church regularly only if it is relevant to their felt needs.
- If they have dropped out of church, they did so because of a bad experience.

Another survey of the unchurched found they didn't attend church services for these four main reasons: (1) Church is too boring and doesn't relate to where I live; (2) I've never been invited; (3) Churches are too interested in my money; and (4) I've been "church damaged" somewhere else. With these multiple perspectives and concerns of the unchurched, finding and keeping their attention can be quite challenging.

There is also the sense that you are already one down when unchurched guests show up for the first time, particularly when they attend alone. The typical first-time attendee attitude is "OK, so I'm here. Impress me if you can." And it's understood that if you can't, he or she won't be back. Many times it seems that an unchurched person is just looking for a reason not to come back.

As our service began that particular Sunday morning with Randy sitting on the back row, I found myself watching the progression of the hour through the eyes of this apprehensive first-time guest. In a new way, I grew even more comfortable with the flow and progression of our service, experiencing it through his resistance. And slowly his body language revealed that he was beginning to lower his defenses as well.

In my heart I began praying for the Lord's direction in the message. How can I present the gospel in a relevant way so as to impact and not overwhelm this young man—and the other hurting and wounded seekers like him?

After the service was over, Randy shook my hand and said he had enjoyed the message that day. He came back several Sundays in a row and usually sat by himself but listened carefully each week. Gradually I could see that he was becoming more comfortable with the idea of attending church.

A few weeks later, Randy brought his wife, Rhonda, and their young son back to our service. We set up weekly meetings to discuss his spiritual journey and answer his questions. Several months later Randy came to my office for our weekly meeting and showed me a little card he had been carrying from Alcoholics Anonymous with the sinner's prayer on it. He told me with great emotion that he had prayed that prayer at the end of our service the previous Sunday and that something had happened in his life. We had an extra-long meeting that week as we began to open up the truths of the Scriptures and work through the normal questions of a new believer.

Miracles of God's grace can still happen.

From this experience and many others like it, we are learning several things about shaping faith in the lives of those who worship with us each week. When a local church can coordinate its efforts for evangelism with the needs of the unchurched, dynamic stories of faith begin to take shape. And when the congregation can enter into this partnership of inviting and attracting into this kind of ministry setting those who are spiritual seekers, miracles of God's grace can happen.

The following list of suggestions is for a church to consider in partnering more effectively with its people to win those who need the Lord.

1. Create opportunities and reasons to invite seekers to your church.

One of the most fruitful efforts a church can make in winning their community is planning an event or activity that believers can invite their unchurched friends and family to attend. Many times by attending with a friend or relative, the unchurched are less critical of a church. Any kind of "bridging event" will do, from a concert or special holiday service to a churchwide picnic that everyone can enjoy. These "bridging" events are designed to create a reason for the regular church attenders to invite their unchurched loved ones. While an evangelistic challenge may not always be a formal part of the event, contacts are made and a major barrier is broken by having these guests attend for the first time. With this friendship approach to evangelism, we build relationships and earn the right to share and shape faith later on in their lives.

2. Remove as many of the barriers in coming to faith as you possibly can.

As a church, we hope to create an experience of coming to church and eventually coming to the Lord with as few hindrances as possible. Of course, we can't lower our standards for faith or compromise what we believe about Christian living. But the environment of grace is necessary for reaching spiritual seekers. We make grace and mercy a high value in the context of reaching the unchurched, trying to reflect God's mercy in giving us what we need rather than what we deserve. As we learn to start where people are, we can move them toward faith in Jesus Christ more effectively. As we respond to their questions and spiritual needs, present the claims of Christ, and love them unconditionally, we can "doubtless come again with rejoicing" (Ps. 126:6, KJV), bringing them to know the Lord.

The church reflects God's mercy—giving us what we need rather than what we deserve.

3. Remember that shaping faith is a process as well as a crisis.

Accepting Jesus Christ into our hearts is a definite crisis, just like being born physically. We all can trace our date of birth to a specific day and time. But the formation and development of personal faith occurs over time, just like the months of growth and prenatal development before a baby is born. Too many times we forget that most of us had to work through several spiritual stick points before we became Christians. Part of our challenge in sharing faith is to help seekers be aware of their spiritual issues and questions, and then help to work through them together. This can be a demanding and lengthy process, but just as rewarding as challenging. Most of the time this trek is best completed on the arm of a close and trusted friend.

4. Prepare each part of the service with the seeker in mind.

Just as I watched Randy during that first church service, most of us would benefit from the practice of watching our church services through the eyes of a first-time guest. Imagine never being to your church before and trying to understand everything that's happening. To get the full impact of this principle, on your next vacation visit a church that you're unfamiliar with. Simple things we take for granted every week in our services will take on a new complexity. Normal things can become very perplexing, like walking in the right door, when to stand and sit in the service, or trying to decide if we should participate in the worship of Communion if we're not members.

By becoming more aware of each announcement, song, and how we do prayer, we can assist the seeker in feeling more comfortable in our church service—and eventually more at ease in coming to faith in Christ.

5. Equip members of your congregation to function in the areas of their strengths and abilities.

The use of spiritual gifts is effective not only for the edification of the church but also for the expanding the body of believers. In other words, sharing our faith can be done in conjunction with the mixture of our set of spiritual gifts. Teachers can teach with the concern for sharing and shaping faith in their listeners. Those with the gift of helps or service can assist others and in the process lead them closer to faith in Christ. In fact, all the spiritual gifts have the potential of being used both inside and outside the Body of Christ, both to share faith with a seeker and shape faith in the believer.

Several of the ladies in our new church are very gifted in arts, painting and making home crafts. Craft shows and handicrafts are quite popular in our area, with craft classes being held in a number of settings in the valley. These faith-filled visionaries have started "craft classes" for the church to invite their friends and neighbors to attend once a month. An admission fee is charged for each class, with the amount based on the cost for the particular project. Profits from the classes go to cover materials for our children in their Sunday School classes. Some of the classes have had more than 40 ladies enrolled, with half of them unchurched women from our community. The church ladies are hostesses at the various tables. During the two to three hours of visiting, they're able to bring up the subject of church life and their faith.

The truth is that we're all more effective in sharing and shaping faith when we function on the basis of our spiritual gift mixes. Far too many believers have been burned out on the thought of personal evangelism simply because they've been taught that faith sharing has to be done a certain way. Find out what you love to do, what you do well, and use it to build a bridge of faith to spiritual seekers around you.

We are more effective in sharing and shaping faith when we function on the basis of our spiritual gifts.

6. Develop a flow for sharing and shaping faith in seekers.

Determine in advance the key spiritual milestones in sharing and shaping faith in the lives of others. Think through the significant steps and spiritual signals people will take in moving toward faith in Christ. Prepare your response for each of those spiritual signals you receive from a seeker.

There are several signals the leaders in our congregation watch and listen for to determine a person's spiritual progress and development toward spiritual maturity. While no one is completely predictable, several indicators become more evident.

One of our guidelines is following the acronym of FAMILY. Each of these six steps is a planned response for the signal we receive from a seeker in sharing and shaping faith in his or her life. The F stands for his or her "first visit." The A represents becoming a regular "attender" on Sunday mornings. The M indicates that he or she has attended one of the quarterly membership classes to become a "member" of the church. The I stands for "investor" as he or she begins to support the church with time, talent, and treasure. The L indicates he or she has found a place to be involved and become a "lay minister" in the church's mission. After completing these first five steps, the Y represents the person's "yields" in attracting and winning others who are coming to faith in Christ.

Additionally, other signals reveal these persons' self-identification with faith and the church. Each week we ask attendees to mark a "welcome card" to register with us and let us know who they are. The choices include "first visit," "second visit," "third visit," "regular attendee," "member," and "out-of-town guest." Obviously, we keep records to know who our church members are, but sometimes a fairly new attendee marks his or her card to say that he or she is a member of the church. This is a significant signal to say the person is feeling comfortable with us and considering this as his or her spiritual home. He or she may request a talk with the pastor or inquire on the registration card about one of the church's ministry teams.

Of course, various signals require different responses to be effective in assisting these fellow travelers in their spiritual journey. For the above "membership response" on a card, we either call or send a form letter to introduce a membership class and invite the person to attend the next scheduled session. A major church event is planned for each of the six steps that a seeker takes from being "a spiritual stranger" to being a devoted member of God's family.

Other signals that local church leaders see as signals of spiritual receptivity include

- writing any kind of message on a welcome card for the first time
- inquiring about church membership classes
- questioning the church's teaching and history
- asking for further information
- asking questions about the message
- bringing a guest for the first time
- requesting prayer for themselves or others
- getting involved in a small group
- enrolling in their first Bible study
- asking to be baptized
- giving their first offering
- volunteering for a ministry task
- offering an idea for ministry

The list could go on indefinitely, depending upon the ministry opportunities and invitations a church makes at any given time to seekers. It may be as simple as a first phone call to the church offices during the week or any statement about "our church," referring to their acceptance of the church as their new spiritual home.

The key is to be alert and catch the signals seekers are sending. As you notice their signal, a timely response in kind is most appropriate—returning a phone call, writing back a handwritten letter in response to their comment card from Sunday. Various response letters for the wide variety of signals can assist in their spiritual progression to faith and the church.

7. Organize various small groups in which seekers can build relationships in the church.

Many churches view small groups and ministry teams only for discipling purposes. But one of the greatest ways smaller groups can function is in building relationships with seekers. For most seekers, until they have connected relationally in a congregation, they will not make much progress toward faith in Christ. That's where small groups fit into the picture. Life change occurs in the context of a small group of 8 to 10 people.

Effective congregations focus on developing a number of small groups and ministry teams whose purpose is to connect with the unchurched and build friendships with them before they ever come to church. We've already mentioned the ladies' craft classes as one of those ministries. Other ideas that are commonly used are dinner groups, in which 8 to 10 adults are invited to a potluck meal and an evening of fellowship. Men's softball teams are great for getting a group of unchurched guys connected. A backyard cookout for several families gives the opportunity to meet new friends. Need-oriented seminars and classes have also been helpful to attract and connect with the unchurched in our community. Topics have included financial planning, marriage enrichment, grief and loss workshops, and parenting classes.

Any number of ministries can be designed to open a side door into the church fellowship rather than just depending upon the typical Sunday morning worship service. The more a congregation of believers begins to strategize on how to relationally connect with seekers, the greater their potential to attract and win others to Christ.

The churches most effective in sharing and shaping faith to-day have learned to partner with their people in fulfilling the Great Commission. The task is too great and too important to be done alone. The truth is, as individuals we cannot attract, win, and disciple our unchurched loved ones without our church family assisting us. And our church, no matter how great its ministries and programs, is ineffective in sharing and shaping faith without the help of each involved and committed member.

This partnership for effective evangelism is dynamic. The united effort becomes a truly win-win situation for everyone involved.

14

Welcoming Newcomers into Fellowship

As the church begins to eliminate the barriers of fragmentation, the walls of isolation, the pain of confrontation, and even the laziness of stagnation, new life will begin to flow through the roots of their soul and begin to rejuvenate the spiritual life of the person as a whole.

—Gary McIntosh and Glen Martin
*Finding Them, Keeping Them:
Effective Strategies for Evangelism and
Assimilation in the Local Church*

Lyle

A young lady wrote of her experience as a newcomer to a church:

My husband and I decided we wanted to attend one of the adult Sunday School classes offered by the church we'd begun to attend. We felt a need to become better acquainted with the people of the congregation. Everyone had been friendly to us during the worship service and in the halls. We were excited about the prospects of fellowship we would find in the more intimate setting of a Sunday School class.

We chose a group we thought would have people of our age and interests. As we walked into the class we saw clusters of people standing around the room drinking coffee, chatting, and laughing. Two or three people looked up as we walked in but continued their visiting. We hovered awkwardly near the door.

After what seemed like a long time the teacher came to the front of the room. Suddenly the clusters broke up and everyone found "their" place to sit down. My husband and I moved tentatively toward a couple of empty chairs. As we started to sit down we were told that those chairs were being saved for someone who would be coming into class late.

By now we were the only ones left standing, so we quickly moved to two chairs off to one side. The leader of the class began the class by recalling what a wonderful time they all had at a class party the previous evening. Various ones chimed in with accounts of funny happenings at the party, which were followed by uproarious laughter.

Finally the teacher began the lesson by asking everyone to turn to Hebrews in their Bibles. Everyone followed along the verse-by-verse study—everyone but us, that is, for we had not brought a Bible. At the end of class we hurried out.

Such an unfortunate treatment of new people, innocent as it may be, reminds us to review how we welcome newcomers into fellowship. This process of acceptance is called "assimilation."

Hospitality helps people feel at home in God's family. Assimilation can be likened to biblical hospitality. Hospitality intentionally creates an atmosphere of acceptance; helping people feel at home in God's family. Successful assimilation results in people being invited into friendship structures within the church.

Assimilation happens as people move from their first contact with the church, to a decision to belong to Christ, to becoming an involved member of the Body of Christ.

One person observed, "You know you belong when you're needed and appreciated." Assimilating people into the fellowship involves creating an atmosphere of warmth and comfort. We must communicate love and acceptance. In one sense we the church do not define assimilation. The outsider does. So while the church may do the right things—for instance, display a friendly attitude—the real issue is "How do people feel about their relationship with us?"

Although incorporation and assimilation are interrelated,

there is a difference. Assimilation is a more intimate step in the process, as follows:

In the process of *incorporation,* newcomers—
Feel socially comfortable in the church.
May be moving toward a salvation experience.
Display openness to questions and answers.
Have a positive first impression of the church.
May not be missed nor turned to for advice.
Have few friends and acquaintances.
Tend to worship and to observe only.

In the process of *assimilation,* newcomers—
Feel accepted into the fellowship of believers.
Are building a trusting relationship.
Are embracing the gospel.
Are appointed by church leaders to chair a committee, to serve as greeter, to give an opinion.
Are missed when absent.
Are sensing oneness and integration with the congregation.
Usually have five to seven friends in church and are involved in a friendship circle.
Are ministering in meaningful tasks.

Incorporation is important and preliminary to assimilation. We dare not stop, however, with the preliminaries of incorporation. We must assimilate people into our fellowship.

Basics of assimilation:

Many churches tend to be inclusive in evangelism but exclusive in relationships. One day I was shocked to hear a man say, "I wish I hadn't gotten saved." When I probed as to what he meant, he said, "Everyone paid attention to me when they wanted to see me get right with God. Now that I've accepted Jesus and attend church regularly, they don't pay attention to me."

This man's church had a mistaken idea of assimilation.

Assimilation begins with the acknowledgment of the human need for belonging.

Assimilation begins with the acknowledgment of the human need for belonging. The church has the wonderful privilege

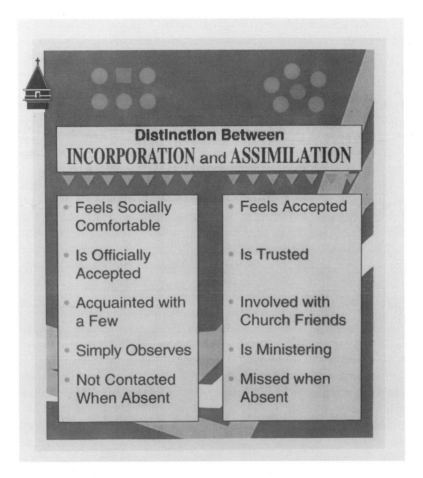

of extending itself to include the new prospect, who at some point feels the uneasiness of being a stranger.

Creating an environment of belonging involves fostering an atmosphere of trust that's reinforced by loving and supportive people. Most of us measure our sense of belonging in a group by how much trust is placed in us. When people turn to newcomers for advice or information, it strengthens their sense of belonging and acceptance.

Assimilation nurtures the fruits of evangelism. When people accept Jesus Christ as Savior, they become part of the Body of Christ. While that's true theologically, it may not be true socially.

We must give attention to making certain that people are included socially. New converts who don't find friendship support often stop attending church functions and eventually drop out altogether. The church must become an extended family to new converts. New believers, recently separated from a sinful life, need help to acquire new behavior patterns. As the old patterns are left behind, past friends may avoid the new believer. A new group is needed to surround them and fill the gap.

While this principle is true, occasionally outsiders resist becoming part of a new group of friends, as did my friend Gene, who attended my young adult Sunday School class. The class members had done all the right things to make him feel accepted. But Gene's own inner sense of unworthiness put up a barrier between him and God's people who welcomed his friendship. "They have it all together," he said, "and here I am a convict. They won't accept me." When pre-Christians bring inner defenses, God's people need to make a diligent effort to build bridges of friendship and love so that trust increases.

Effective assimilation views new converts as disciples in process rather than mere newcomers to the faith. We must take them in right where they are and not place expectations on them that don't take into account their spiritual infancy.

Assimilation is more than getting people to formally join the church. People who join drop out after a few months and become what we call "dead wood" unless they are brought into the life, fellowship, and ministry of the church. Dead wood may, in fact, be an indictment against the church. Our relationship with the newcomer must be more than a formal sponsorship.

People come to church seeking relationships.

People come to church seeking relationships. Effective assimilation happens when the new convert has friends in the church. When a newcomer reports to me, "Oh, sure —I know several people in your church," I figure that person is more apt to return as a worshiper, because he or she undoubtedly has repeated exposures to the congregation's beliefs, expectations, and personnel.

Most people new to church have likely experienced some dislocation or problem in their lives. *We must expect to pay the cost of time and energy to assimilate them.* God has probably worked through some troubling factor in their lives to bring them to the place of seeking Him. The stressful aspects of their lives have opened their hearts to the church's ministry and to God's working. We must attempt to discern and understand.

A pastor friend of mine responded to the cost of assimilation with a grin and said, "I'm weary." We know how he feels. The assimilation process is indeed demanding—but rewarding. A person in a church new to him or her must make a lot of adjustments understanding new beliefs and learning the traditions and ways of a particular congregation. These factors impede the development of new relationships without the deliberate, loving attention of a caring congregation.

Assimilation must be intentional. Relationship evangelism reminds us that we are to grow disciples, not just to secure decisions. Two factors require persistent attention. First, decision-focused evangelism tends to encourage dropouts. Once the decision has been made, we feel our goal has been accomplished. If the person does not stick with Jesus, we're inclined to say, "He [or she] probably wasn't serious to begin with." But a decision to follow Christ requires the nurture of fellow believers. Decision-focused evangelism needs to be replaced with disciple-making evangelism.

We are to grow disciples, not just to secure decisions.

Second, most established churchgoers seldom give thought to the need for assimilation. They don't remember that someone paid a high price in energy to involve and incorporate them when *they* first began attending church. Probably someone initially befriended them and sustained the friendship. Church members need to be reminded: assimilation is never automatic.

Because new converts may seem to threaten the existing social structures in the local church, assimilation should be approached on an individual basis. People satisfied with their friendship circles will not be open to new people.

In the church foyer one day I was startled to hear a man say, "Now that the Joneses have moved, we have room in our Sunday School class for two more people." He had no awareness of how snooty and exclusive his comment sounded. Rather, he was grieving the loss of his close friends. His social circle had been disrupted, and he felt the need to replenish the loss with new friends.

Someone—the pastor, Sunday School superintendent, Sunday School teacher, or class greeter—should introduce visitors to groups where receptive people will draw them in and help them get acquainted. We do well to consider which groups have the most in common with each prospect. Personality types may also be factored into matching people with each other. In the Sunday School or the church, a discerning person or couple should be assigned this task of uniting prospects with appropriate groups.

Effective assimilation does not demand massive programs, sophisticated classes, and many workers. A hospitable church simply requires members genuinely care for people until a self-sustaining feeling of belonging is developed.

Assimilation must be a preconversion, as well as a postconversion, process. We sow the seed of the gospel generously to bring about a significant harvest. Multiple contacts with believers and repeated exposure to the gospel increase the opportunity for people to be successfully assimilated into the Kingdom.

Consider assimilation as a process illustrated by these steps: an outsider begins to attend, becomes a new believer, participates in a group, joins the church as a member, involves himself as a worker, reproduces himself spiritually by winning someone to Jesus Christ. While these steps may not occur in a specific order, each should lead a person toward greater involvement and commitment.

Church should be a place where an atmosphere of love for the lost prevails. Certain behavior patterns among Christians determine the climate of the local church, which is quickly discerned by new people. The atmosphere of a church either draws or repels. In a hospitable church, the people who make the first impression, such as greeters and ushers, will not simply perform their assigned tasks of shaking hands, passing out bulletins, or collecting the offering. They must genuinely care for people, and in the performance of their duties be sensitive to the needs and feelings of outsiders.

A united congregation that genuinely encounters God in worship attracts unbelievers.

A church that prays for lost people generally accepts unbelievers just as they are. A minis-

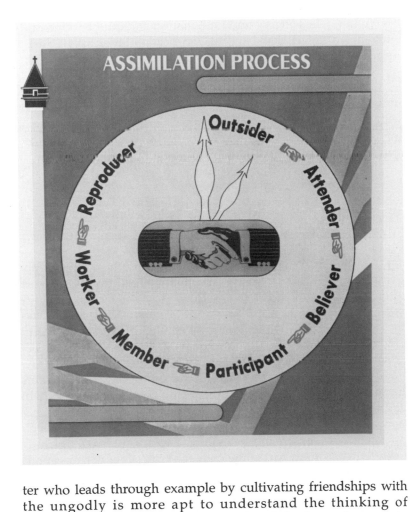

ter who leads through example by cultivating friendships with the ungodly is more apt to understand the thinking of unchurched people. Similarly, lay church leaders who seek to perpetuate contacts outside their church will be more aware of ministry opportunities. Leaders, too, will select programs, plans, procedures, and priorities addressing the issues and concerns of outsiders. These leaders condition the climate of a church.

A united congregation that genuinely encounters God in worship attracts unbelievers. The expression of joy in the Lord during and following worship services will be evident to them.

Actually less energy and imagination is required to incorporate a new believer than is necessary to win him or her to Christ. Assimilation is well worth the effort.

The Church's task in assimilating new converts:

1. *Contact.* Making contacts and cultivating friendships with unbelievers is the first step in preevangelism—a lifestyle in which we keep in touch with people during the daily routine of living. We build relationships. Assimilation begins as we get acquainted and nurture a friendship.

2. *Conversion.* In this step we introduce the Good News. We have brought the prospect to the point of receiving Christ. Now it is time to introduce him or her to the family of God.

3. *Nurture faith.* We teach the rudimentary concepts of Christian life. We encourage new believers to pray, worship, study the Bible, fellowship, serve, tithe, and witness.

4. *Body life.* While one-on-one discipleship is a popular slogan and approach to ministry, assimilation into the larger body of believers is limited by that method. Instead, encourage every person to move into a group. Sunday School, for example, has the potential to be a wonderfully welcoming organization. Every new believer needs to begin developing a support network beyond just one or two persons.

5. *Membership.* At this juncture, the appropriate person offers information to the new convert regarding church membership. In addition to teaching him or her the doctrines of the denomination, a historical sketch of the local church helps the person develop a sense of identity and belonging. Explain ways by which he or she can become a part of the ongoing life of your congregation.

6. *Ministry assignment.* A job in the church paves an avenue of acceptance for new members. Not every task in the church is open to new converts, but many ministry opportunities are within the comfort zone of most newcomers, including those of ushers, greeters, and membership on certain committees or in the choir. Serving God gives newcomers the opportunity to be an important part of the body life.

An awareness of the "don'ts" can be as essential to the assimilation process as the "dos." The following list will help caring church members be more sensitive to the needs of newcomers. Avoid:

- *Controlling family networks.* Networks can be wonderful caring units—when they don't make new people feel like outsiders. Members of family networks already have a sense of belonging and may not realize the newcomer needs that same feeling. If a person is on the inside of a network, he or she sees it is as a cozy cluster. But the newcomer, outside the family network, may perceive the group as a cold and uncaring clique.

- *Facilities that discourage interaction.* In church buildings, the structure can work against fellowship. If possible, find ways to expand a small foyer, create a room large enough to be a fellowship hall, and provide a kitchen big enough to prepare church dinners comfortably.

- *Tradition that dwells on "the good old days" and lives in the past.* Every church has some very special past experiences. Longtime members may assume everyone knows and appreciates that rich tradition. But newcomers probably know little or nothing about a particular church's history. Introduce the history and tradition of your church to new members at the proper time in an acceptable way, realizing that the future may look much different from the past.

- *An atmosphere of strife.* A reputation of friction will repel newcomers. Seekers are not attracted by conflict and backbiting.

- *Worship styles that are difficult for the uninitiated to understand.*

- *A no-growth attitude.* "Our church is big enough already."

- *Economic or social differences.* While the gospel includes everyone, not everyone is comfortable with economic or social differences. While we're not talking primarily about racial differences, I remember bringing an African-American man to a large church of about 2,100 worshipers. Looking over the congregation of all white attendees, he mused, "I'm the only one here today." Because there were no other Blacks, he felt alone among 2,100 other worshipers. The same reaction can take place when people observe economic distance between themselves and the majority of the congregation.

- *Noncommitment.* Some people recoil from commitment to anything. Our culture has imprinted the baby boomers, for instance, with a fear of attaching to any person, cause, or organization. This mentality can be an excuse to avoid responsibility.

- *Nontrust.* A feeling on the part of the established church members that "We can't trust these new people. They may ruin our church."
- *Feelings of inferiority* on the part of church members.

The following seven recommendations are based on the assumption that relationships are more important than processes:

- Identify newcomers in nonthreatening ways.
- Look at your church through the eyes of a first-time visitor. What needs to change? Evaluate frequently.
- Train people to welcome newcomers before greeting their regular friends. This does not require that church members disdain existing friendships, which are often the result of effective assimilation anyway. Greeting newcomers first reflects sensitivity.
- Provide visitors with words to songs and scripture. Involve them in all activities.
- Help newcomers find small groups to study in, to sing with, to play alongside. The Sunday School, Bible studies, the choir, or sports teams are wonderful ways to include people.
- Consider individualizing the assimilation process. Look for the kinds of people who will give themselves to new people, and match them up with newcomers.
- Start new groups. When new groups begin, they open the congregation to new people. Approach two to six people about pioneering a new Sunday School class, a Bible study, or a hospitality ministry. Provide them with a list of prospects. Ask them to pray about this opportunity. (Even if the new group is not started, the needs and the importance of outsiders are highlighted.) When creating new groups, avoid dividing a class or interfering with friendships.

Steve and Anita Arnold moved into town and decided to try Calvary Church because two young couples invited them to the New Beginnings Sunday School class. When Steve and Anita came to church, they were warmly greeted by friendly individuals who opened doors and provided directions to the Sunday School class-

room. Once in the classroom, a host and hostess served them doughnuts and coffee. They were introduced to the class members. The teacher inquired about their recent move, the fact they were looking for a church home, and their job situation. Steve and Anita, already Christians, quickly spoke of their relationship with God.

The Arnolds later brought Rod and Connie, friends of theirs from Denver. "We found such warmth and openness at Calvary that we never considered going elsewhere," they said. "We wanted Rod and Connie to experience the same caring we encountered."

This response is the norm in healthy, growing churches. Every hospitable church wants to welcome new people.

15

How Is Faith Formed in Us?

Everyone who hears these words of mine and puts them into practice is like a wise man who built his house on the rock.
—Matt. 7:24

Jim

For the past few weeks we've watched in horror as houses in our area of southern California have been sliding off the sides of mountains. A few had been teetering on the edge of the chasm beneath them as the land has continued to erode away, leaving their foundations hanging in thin air. Some neighbors have captured their final plunge on home video and made the national news as these expensive homes were destroyed in one thunderous crash.

Although the owners had purchased their dream homes and beautiful view lots with different expectations, nature had an incredible way of revealing their property's weaknesses. There is no way to adequately describe the sense of loss and disappointment of these unfortunate families.

Faith is to be our strong and secure foundation in life's tough times.

While the owners had no doubt invested in their homes in many visible ways, it was the unseen problems with the foundation and the land they stood on that eventually took their toll on the properties. All the exterior aesthetics meant little when the homes rolled down the slopes and splintered into a pile of debris.

The Scriptures teach that our lives can be like that, having the appearance of being strong and well only to have the facade come crashing down in the storms of life. Faith needs to be our strong and secure foundation in the tough times.

Listen to these descriptions of faith:

The fundamental fact of existence is that this trust in God, this faith, is the firm foundation under everything that makes life worth living. It's our handle on what we can't see (Heb. 11:1, TM).

Faith makes us sure of what we hope for and gives us proof of what we cannot see (Heb. 11:1, CEV).

It is the nature of faith

● to give hope for the future
● to provide focus and a reason to believe
● to bring confidence and assurance
● to develop certainty for our future
● to grow and become stronger
● to be contagious and influence others

Faith is foundational to our Christian life. Faith brings us into connection with God then leads us into connection with others. As we share our faith with those around us, it is especially important that we understand the processes by which faith is formed. The Scriptures have a great deal to say on the subject.

The Main Focus Factor

The Lord taught us the importance of understanding the purpose and priority of faith in our lives. In the Sermon on the Mount, Jesus preached, *But first be concerned about his kingdom and what has his approval. Then all these things will be provided for you* (Matt. 6:33, GW).

Faith holds to a set of values for life, a mission and purpose for this world. Authentic faith places a priority on the eternal and keeps a balanced perspective on what is really important. Faith always suffers when it has the wrong focus.

The apostle Paul described faith's "Main Focus Factor" in Rom. 12:2, when he wrote,

Don't become so well-adjusted to your culture that you fit into it without even thinking. Instead, fix your attention on God. You'll be changed from the inside out (Rom. 12:2, TM).

Fixing our attention on God keeps us safe from the pressures and problems of life. Rather than be overly worried about the normal demands of the day-to-day, we can look above it all and fix our attention on the Lord. This "main focus factor" can be transformational to faith.

The Envisioning Factor

The faith chapter defines faith as knowing what we do not see. The *God's Word* translation reads like this

Faith assures us of things we expect and convinces us of the existence of things we cannot see (Heb. 11:1, GW).

The Living Bible says it like this:

What is faith? It is the confident assurance that something we want is going to happen. It is the certainty that what we hope for is waiting for us, even though we cannot see it up ahead (Heb. 11:1, TLB).

As we dream and imagine what God can do, our faith grows.

As we begin to dream and imagine what God can do, our faith begins to grow. The ability to envision the unseen is what faith is. This is especially important to the work of evangelism. Life sometimes has a way of draining our dreams. The troubles of life can nearly beat faith right out of us!

At times we really don't have to do anything to lose a strong faith—by neglecting our spiritual life we can nullify our faith.

By cultivating a dream, we can begin to exercise our faith. One of my faith exercises is to get away once in a while and begin to use the God-given imagination for forming faith in my own heart. The more we can learn to envision, the more our faith will grow and expand.

This past year I had the rare opportunity to hear in person Paul Cho, pastor of the largest Christian congregation in the world. At last count his church, located in Seoul, had 750,000 members. He said God had given him a new dream—for 1 million members. He then said something about envisioning faith that we realize is so true: "At first God will give us a dream. . . . As we nurture and care for it, something transformational begins to happen. . . . As we begin, we have a dream. But then—the dream has us!"

Faith captures our heart. As we guard our affections, faith becomes captivating. Many say, "I'll have to see it to believe it," as Thomas said of our risen Lord. But people of faith who develop the envisioning factor learn to say, "Believe it, and you'll see it"!

Now, if all we use is our imagination and stop there, we're just dreamers. So then we move on to another phase of forming our faith.

The Resistance Factor

Any person of faith can expect to experience some opposition. It's true throughout the Scriptures, and we experience it in life and in our efforts to evangelize as well. Eventually mature faith begins to expect some opposition.

We never need to be anxious about the opposition. We only need to be aware of our protection. When we read the faith chapter, we find the great people of faith were outnumbered many times—but faith in God helped overcome the odds.

Faith refuses to count the enemies or consider all the obstacles and problems. Faith is formed within us, not by looking at the measurable externals. Forming faith is an inside job. Read again of some of these heroes in Heb. 11—

They were protected from lions, fires, and sword thrusts, turned disadvantage to advantage, won battles, routed alien armies (vv. 33-34, TM).

There is a sense of divine protection when we fix our attention on God, keep the eternal values as our highest priority, and move into any resistance with an awareness of His care.

The Stepping-Stone Factor

As a child I joined other children in hiking the meadows and farms in southern Ohio. Often we were able to cross the streams by rolling larger stones into the water and making our way one stepping-stone at a time.

Faith builds on our previous experiences in much the same way. Each victory enables us to trust God for more. Each person we see come to faith gives us the courage to believe for others. Each answer to prayer and miracle is an encouragement to move farther along in the process of faith.

The apostle Paul described this "stepping-stone factor" in forming faith when he wrote the words of 2 Cor. 1:5—

Indeed, experience shows us that the more we share in Christ's immeasurable suffering the more we are able to give of his encouragement (PHILLIPS).

Just as problems can be viewed as an obstacle to faith, they can also be seen as stepping-stones in our spiritual formation. It's all in how you look at it. Jesus said it this way: *According to your faith be it unto you* (Matt. 9:29, KJV). Our faith can interpret our experiences in life as stepping-stones or stumbling blocks— that's really up to us!

Faith grows as it views life from God's vantage point. Resistance and problems, obstacles and challenges can make or break our faith, but it's our responsibility to view them from the right perspective. Faith grows as it views life from God's vantage point and His eternal perspective. The overwhelming problems we experience today will seem insignificant many years from now. Our faith will be able to move us on to a greater level of trust and confidence. God working through us can provide a greater spiritual result than we imagined.

The Fervency Factor

One of the myths of forming faith is that it involves *only* believing. Some have misunderstood that faith grows as we wait passively before God and expect Him to rescue us in each crisis. But that's a dangerous extreme.

The Bible clearly teaches that believing and doing must go together. In fact, that's the point of the parable of the wise man building his house upon the rock—"hearing these sayings, and doing them." Faith is formed through obedient action. Faith cannot survive without obedience and putting truth into practice.

When will you ever learn that "believing" is useless without doing what God wants you to? Faith that does not result in good deeds is not real faith (James 2:20, TLB). Let's involve ourselves in the lives of others— telling them about Jesus, giving them gifts, encouraging their hearts.

Edward McGrath Jr. tells a story of acting on faith that involved a little boy who wanted to play baseball but was physically unable. The little guy said, "I'm not old enough to play baseball or football. I'm not eight yet. My mom told me that when I start baseball I won't be able to run that fast because I had an operation. I told Mom I wouldn't need to run that fast. When I play baseball, I'll just hit them out of the park—then I'll be able to walk."

What a great expression of faith!

The Less-Is-More Factor

Many times people of faith discover that less is more.

In a day when simplifying is the trend, downward mobility is in style, and everyone longs for an uncomplicated lifestyle, the walk of faith reminds us that less with God is always more than we would have on our own.

Martin Luther arose early every day for an hour of prayer. But he said that if he had a very busy day planned, he would have to get up earlier and pray for two or three hours. That's the perspective of a person of faith. Most of us would allow the busy schedule to completely crowd out any devotional and prayer time, but the person of faith knows that "less is more."

Believers are challenged to give the first 10 percent to God as an act of worship and an expression of faith in Him. Each week the offering plate is passed down the row at church, it is a test of faith to obey God and trust Him to provide for our needs. When we return to God the first 10 percent of our income, and trust Him to care for our needs with the other 90 percent remaining, we're practicing this faith factor. Any mature believer will declare, "I can't afford *not* to tithe!" Why? Because with God less is more! He can do more with the remaining 90 percent than we could ever do with the 100 percent if we kept it all for ourselves!

Studying the Scriptures we find some incredible stories to illustrate this faith-forming factor. God told Gideon's army, "You can't go to battle yet—you have too many soldiers." He used a one-man army in Samson to astound the enemies of Israel. Jesus called the most unlikely crowd to be His followers and establish the work of the Kingdom in this world. In fact, God intentionally selects the weak to confound the strong, and the simple to surprise the wise—because faith knows less is more!

The fascinating process God continues to use in forming faith in us and through us does not fit into any of this natural world's standards. His ways are above our ways. The challenge for us is to stay in tune with the moving of His Spirit around us. Watch and see what God is doing, and try to become a part of it.

Together as we enter into this adventure, we can discover the new things God is doing around us and in us for shaping and sharing our faith.